PERFECTING IMPERFECTIONS

By Anupriya Srivastava

Chennai • Bangalore

CLEVER FOX PUBLISHING
Chennai, India

Published by CLEVER FOX PUBLISHING 2024
Copyright © Anupriya Srivastava 2024

All Rights Reserved.
ISBN: 978-93-56482-84-5

This book has been published with all reasonable efforts taken to make the material error-free after the consent of the author. No part of this book shall be used, reproduced in any manner whatsoever without written permission from the author, except in the case of brief quotations embodied in critical articles and reviews.

The Author of this book is solely responsible and liable for its content including but not limited to the views, representations, descriptions, statements, information, opinions and references ["Content"]. The Content of this book shall not constitute or be construed or deemed to reflect the opinion or expression of the Publisher or Editor. Neither the Publisher nor Editor endorse or approve the Content of this book or guarantee the reliability, accuracy or completeness of the Content published herein and do not make any representations or warranties of any kind, express or implied, including but not limited to the implied warranties of merchantability, fitness for a particular purpose. The Publisher and Editor shall not be liable whatsoever for any errors, omissions, whether such errors or omissions result from negligence, accident, or any other cause or claims for loss or damages of any kind, including without limitation, indirect or consequential loss or damage arising out of use, inability to use, or about the reliability, accuracy or sufficiency of the information contained in this book.

Oscillating between flaws and beauty, light and shadow, while perfecting imperfections.

The book's narrative flows through three phases, much like the Japanese philosophy of a Kintsugi vase:

Fragmented, Reparated, Restored.

Perfecting Imperfections embarks on a journey of breaking and making to find one's true self. In a world where flaws and beauty coexist, where light dances with shadow, the quest to find our true selves unfolds. Striving to find perfections in our imperfections, it is a tale of life, love, and young confusion.

FRAGMENTED:
When one's spirit gets fragmented by the trials and tribulations of life, unwrapping their emotions—like a broken vase, flaws and vulnerabilities are exposed, but amidst the chaos, persistence sows seeds of self-discovery.

REPARATED:
The journey progresses and embarks on a path of repair and restoration, just as a skilled artisan meticulously mends the broken shards of a vase with golden lacquer and attempts to heal those wounds and rebuild a sense of self. Through resilience and introspection, slowly gathering the strength to confront those imperfections and embracing the beauty that lies within.

RESTORED:
In the final phase, emerging from the crucible of self-discovery, transformed and resurrected. Like a Kintsugi ceramic, they have been shaped by the mending process, and their once-broken self now radiates a unique and captivating brilliance—in accepting both their flaws and innate beauty, perfecting the imperfections, and becoming whole by embracing authenticity.

Dedications

To hopes and faith unshaken
To ardent beliefs
To Becoming
To Unbecoming
To Life of thousand deaths
To Force and Universe
To that secret little diary
To some unheard sentiments
To emotions slowly becoming prose & poetry
and lastly
To those who believed in me

CONTENTS

FRAGMENTED

1. Timeless
2. Worse Than Grief
3. Take Me Back Home
4. A Muted Sea
5. Ocean Blue Love
6. Purple Mind
7. Scars
8. Void
9. Pieces of Me
10. Seasons

REPARATED

11. Slow Love
12. To Unlove is Love Taking a Step Back
13. Where I Dwell
14. Break Me Apart
15. Prey
16. Shadow Tunnel
17. Grey
18. Black and White
19. Pov Skin
20. The Assembly

RESTORED

21. Mask Unmasked
22. Hate Letter
23. Reignite Hope
24. Perfecting Imperfections
25. Joineries
26. Reminscents
27. To My Ambivalent Demons

FRAGEMENTED

TIMELESS

What I gave was eternal
What I received was temporary
I wanted it to age, die and live forever
In the Universe and space, so endless
Formless, shapeless
I wanted something so timeless

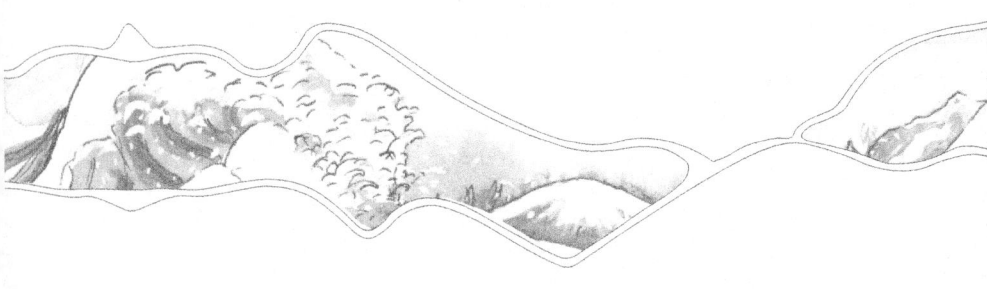

They might not know
what it's like to let it flow
'Coz paddling the boat with a specific destination
Never lets you explore
The unknown shores

Where lies magic,
for don't you know
it's something like an undiscovered bliss
Always there and timeless

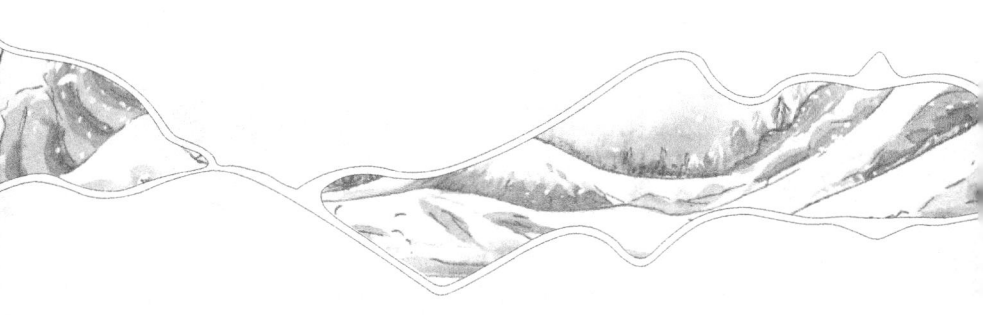

Now, I am left alone
On the banks so distant
I poured my heart out
that it feels so vacant

Unsure of the capabilities to feel again;
For the defeat yet stubborn love, so priceless
Looking straight into their hearts,
Which were merciless

Was it too much to ask?
Us to be timeless.

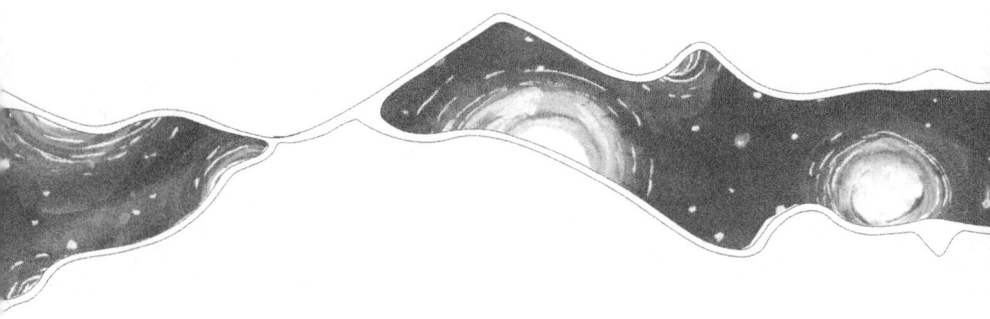

Here, when you come back to say:
"I promise I will change."
When I am on the mend,
Seemingly sorry to see me where I am

Don't feel guilty, as this was never part of the plan;
But now I know it brings me to all my fears,
from which I ran

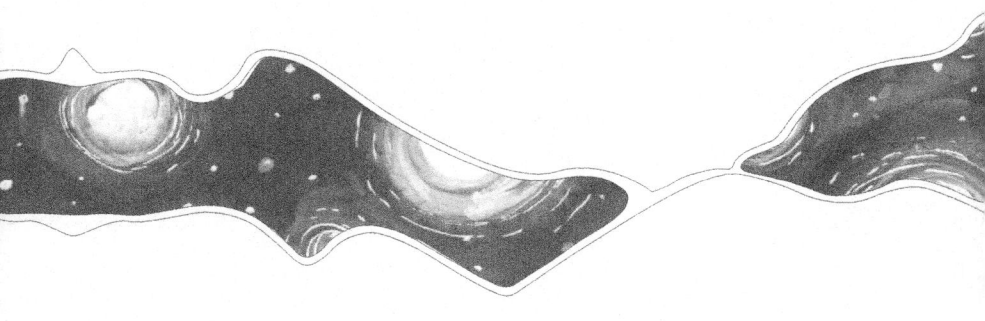

I accidentally got broke,
but divinely so woke
For don't you know,
I got something so endless

I can fall short of words to tell the story,
It's timeless!

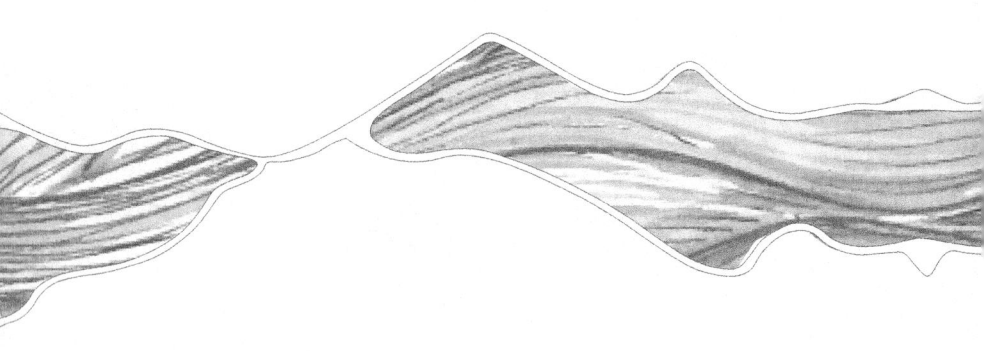

WORSE THAN GRIEF

What's worse than grief?

Grief that goes unrecorded, I wonder
What's best is letting it sink and surrender

Gazing into the enormous sea, so wide
which took all teardrops in its high tide

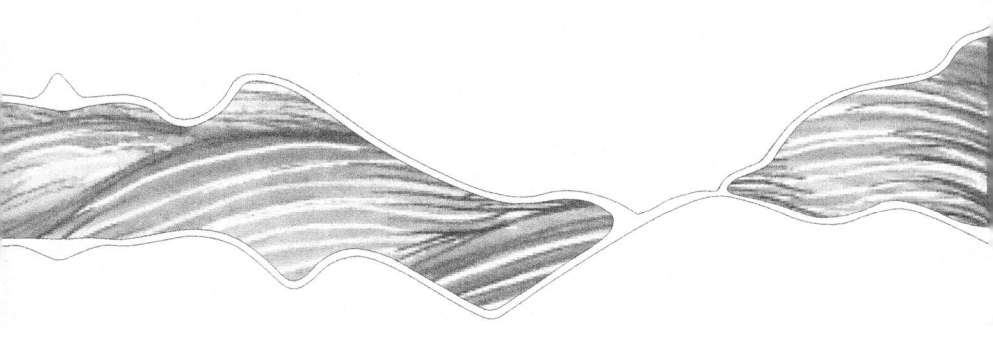

TAKE ME BACK HOME

Take me back to home,
where I can see the stars
whilst lying somewhere safe,
somewhere loved,
somewhere that can contain all of me

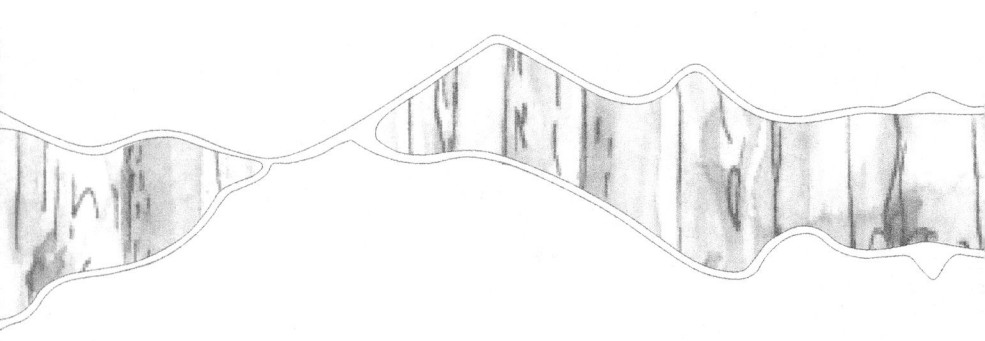

Take me back home,
where the wind blows over my face
my hair dances carefree on its beats
whilst someone caresses my forehead
with their gentle touch

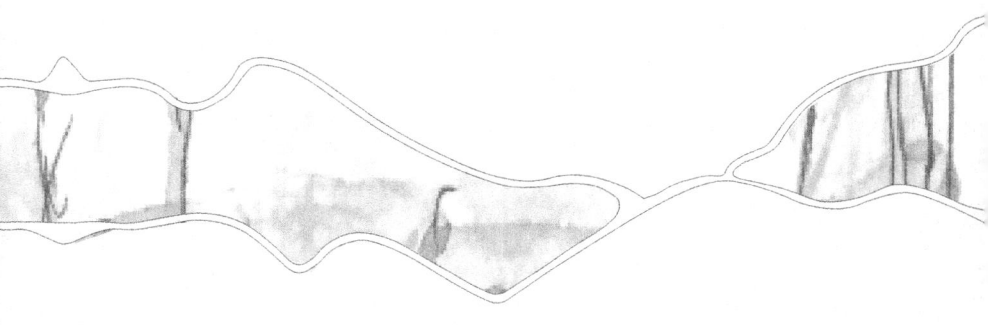

Their fingers on my eyelids
subtly closing them,
and pressing my neck
as if opening the knob of a briefcase
unpacking all the burdens
And I can slowly lie down
in a place of gentle calm
like I have nothing to carry more.

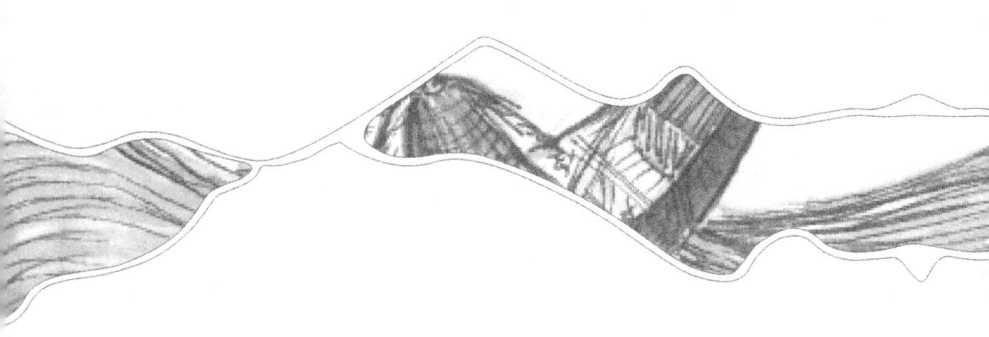

Take me back home,
where the couch is wide enough,
to fit all my dilemmas
as I lie down, rest my face.
Take me back home
where life doesn't feel like
some kind of race.

Take me back home
from where I don't have to leave
To find a better life
where I belong forever.

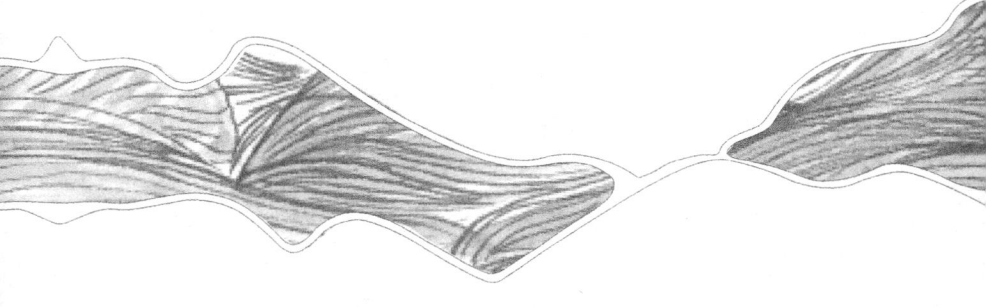

Take me back to home,
where my feet can rest, arms are held,
where someone kisses gently on my forehead,
sings a lullaby to sleep on my bed.

Take me back home,
where someone comes back to me
and says: now, it feels like home.

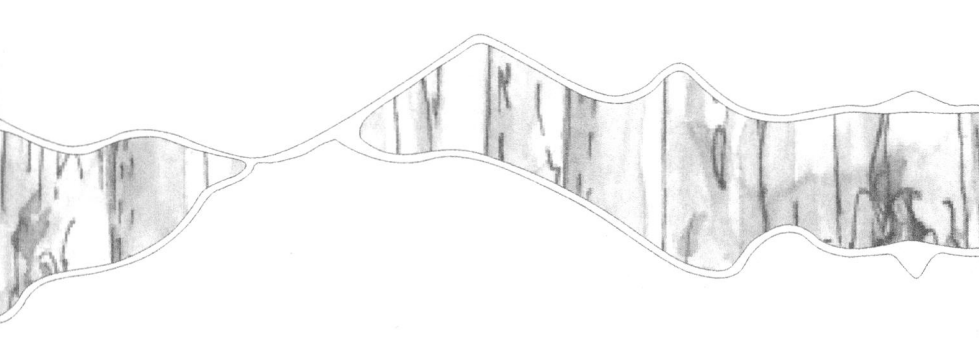

A MUTED SEA

Silently folding, roving within waves
of my own torment,
and all those who turned their back
in the moment;
I was like a muted sea,
shouting but can't be heard;
from the banks so distant.

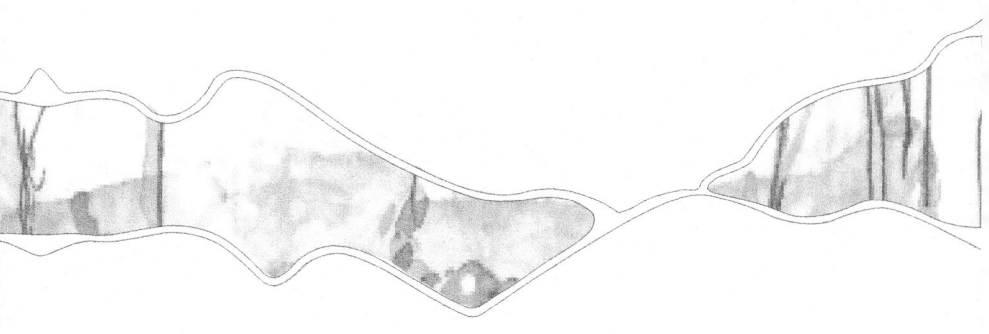

My tears became tide,
and my troubled waters
became a view;
for the watchers,
I was like a muted sea
brimming with grief

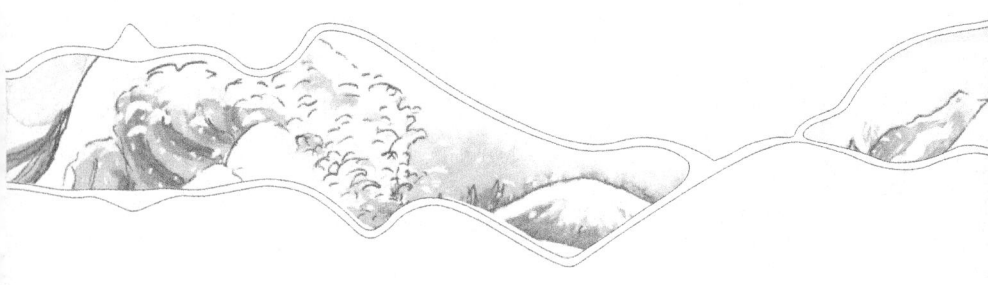

Turmoil went on and on
But they were all busy listening
to their own happy songs.
The waves relentlessly attacked;

One after the other,
Of pain that left ungreeted;
By those who washed
the filth in my blues.

I remember playing with them,
Tickling their toes like a child;
Little did I know I was inviting,
A whole lot of trouble in paradise.

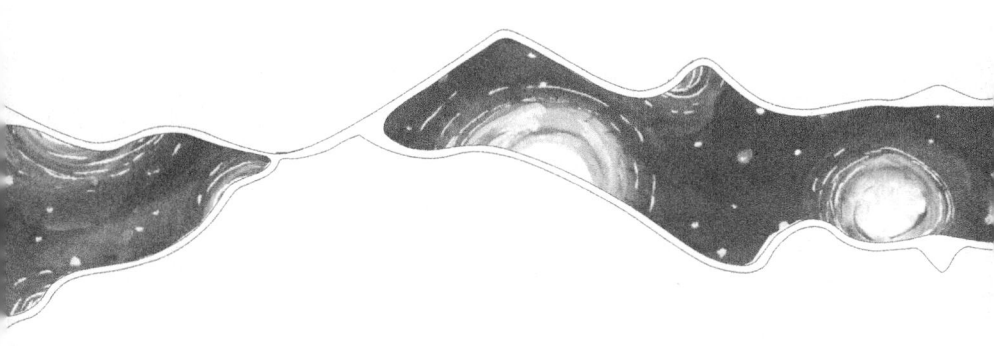

They'll leave the shore,
Once their hearts are full,
I would give my all to entertain,
in the moment so brief;

I was like a muted sea,
brimming with grief.

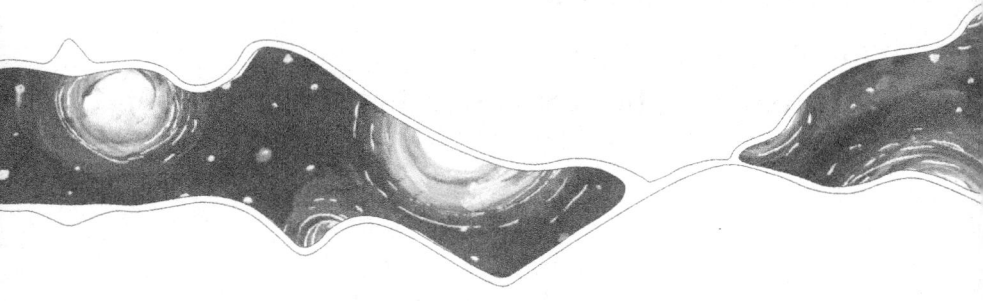

OCEAN BLUE LOVE

The bluish-green waves of the ocean
trying to wash off all the chaos, dilemmas,
slowly, cautiously from off my feet.
Gently touching my body once,
twice and going on & on.

The touch was soothing,
relaxing and healing
To my all inner wounds

Crystal clear soul of the ocean
Whispering some truth
In waves reflecting sunshine
Far from deceptions & worldly lies

In the warm hold of mountains,
him shining and playing
until the moonlight
which strikes in the middle of the night,
where he starts darkening,
Appearing as if shedding some skin
releasing all the tears he had seen.

Burying it all deep down,
hiding it in nightglow
to take rebirth the next morning
to live with the same zeal and flow.

Its endless and vast appearance
to my tiny human existence
will never know its depth or width,
will never know what all it is made up of
And what all it consists of.

His ocean-blue love
Big yet humble,
loud but grounded,
ambiguous but truthful,
scary, but mine.

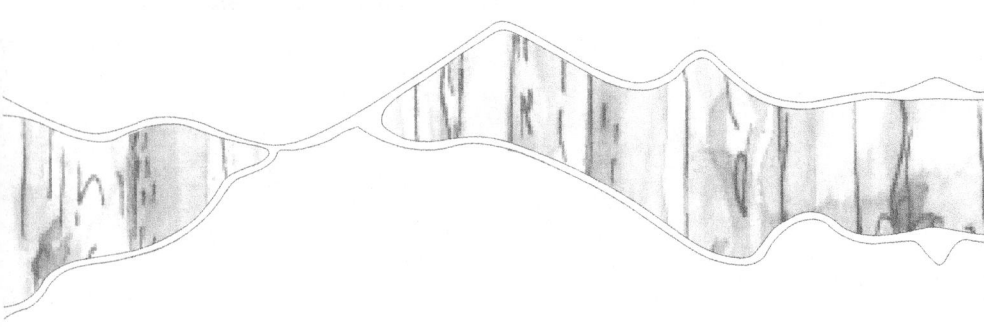

Allegory of his greatness
can never fall short
Watching and staring at him
until I get caught
scared of losing myself in him

I was conflicted by
his ability to seem so destructing
but humbled as it feels so forgiving.

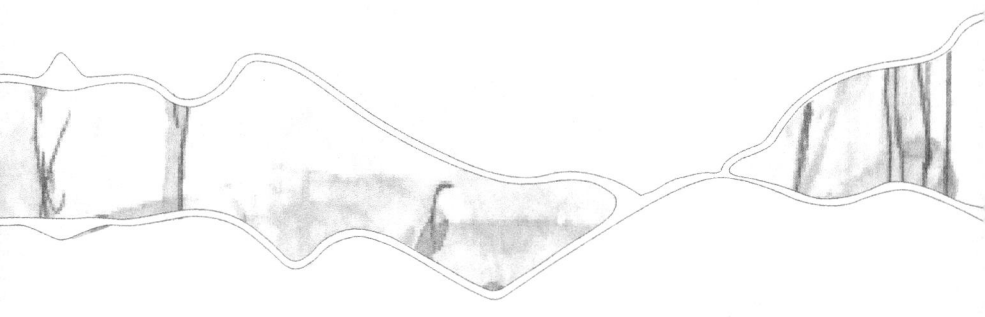

PURPLE MIND

His indecisiveness about staying
or leaving the shore—
a kind of romanticism
I've never ever seen.

He says, "Some form of love
cannot be contained, just lived."
To all his loving lies
I blindly believed

My crimson heart
couldn't help but
paint a picture of the perfect love story
As I slide back
the tray of his memory
under the bed
my purple mind,
somewhere hinting
"His ocean-blue love
might lead me to sink."

Trying to wrap around my head,
Why it's never meant to be "Valentine Red."

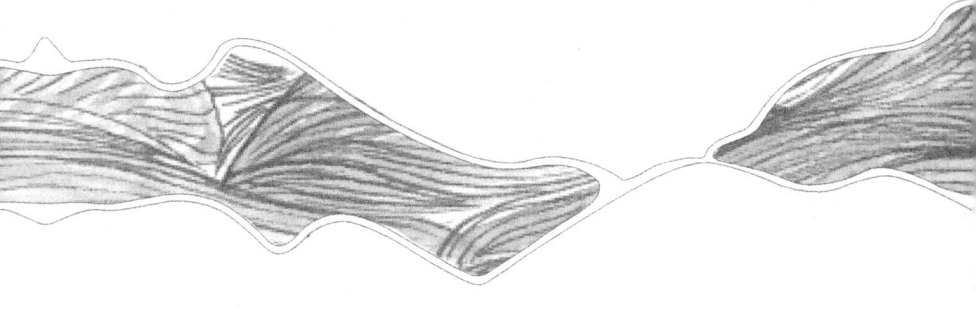

SCARS

Who likes it broken
Who loves your scars?

Because when I see through it,
I have fallen in love with you even more.
Admire how you gave me a tour
to best corners of your soul, completely bare
Inside sacred places and hearts so rare

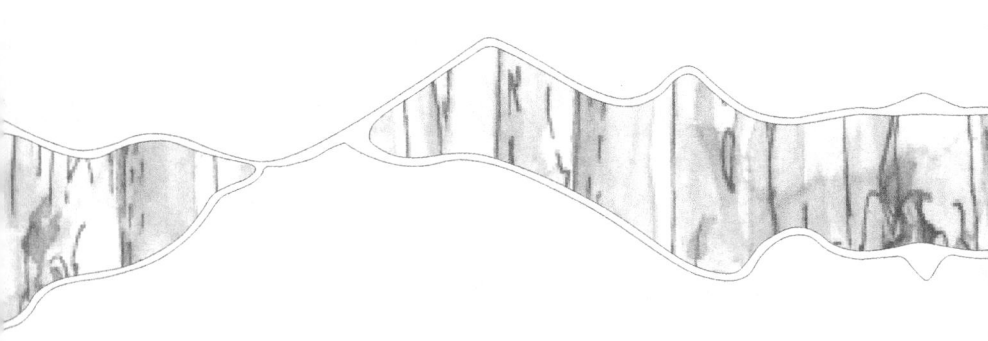

I wonder where the dark abyss is
To measure the pain,
you hid behind that bliss.

You are mistaken if you think,
"I like sunshine."
I was always the moon;
To brighten up the night sky.

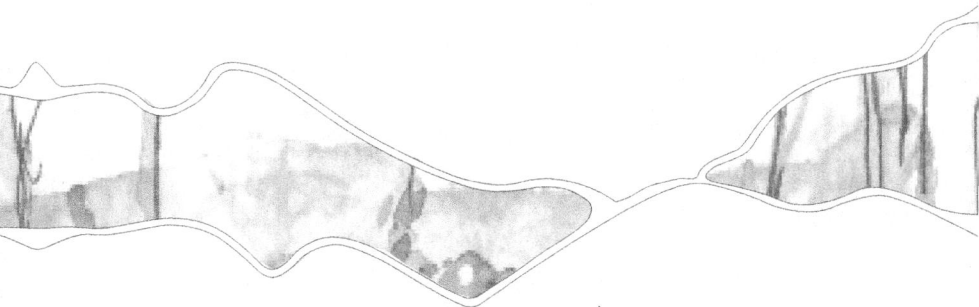

So, don't be scared,
To make me see your flaws,
or the cuts that ripped you apart.
For you being made to love as a whole;
not in just some of your glowing parts.

For the beauty in you gleam
Coming from the Light that's within
And those cracks like a beam
It only shines brighter;
when things around are a little darker

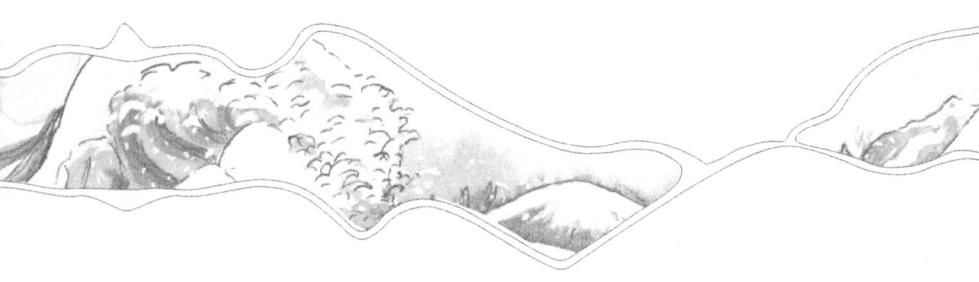

So yes, when I say it, I like it broken
Please don't be mistaken

Let me admire you
for the story that's true,
Perfection, mere a lie, so stark

Your scars, in fact,
are the best beauty marks.

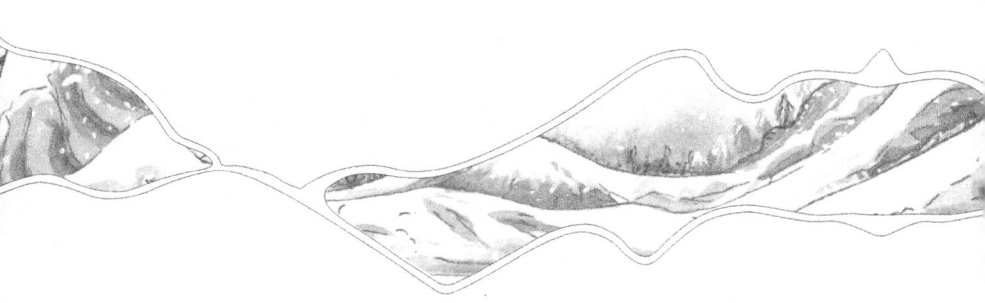

VOID

What we know of nothingness
A feeling of feeling nothing
Or maybe a feeling after you felt everything?
Is it a void aftermath of most things

Or is it a hole?
Endless, hopeless, merciless
like a vacuum
or a deafness after too much noise
I wonder what's nothingness of void.

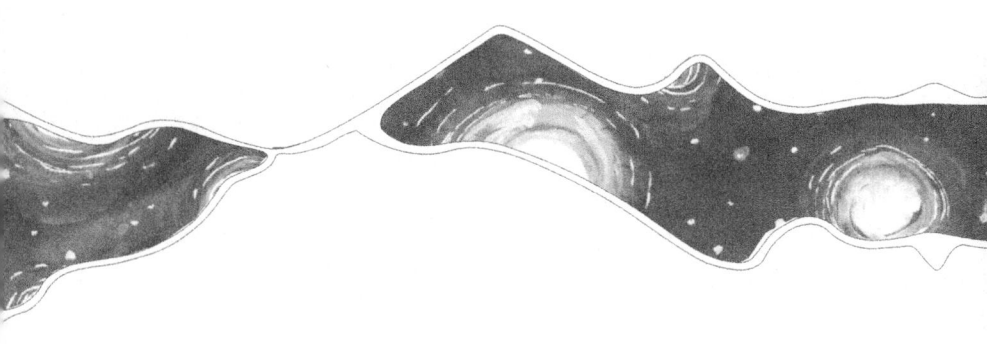

Is it the absence
Or presence
which makes no sense
Is it a fear of being left alone
or is finding no one
in the presence of everyone

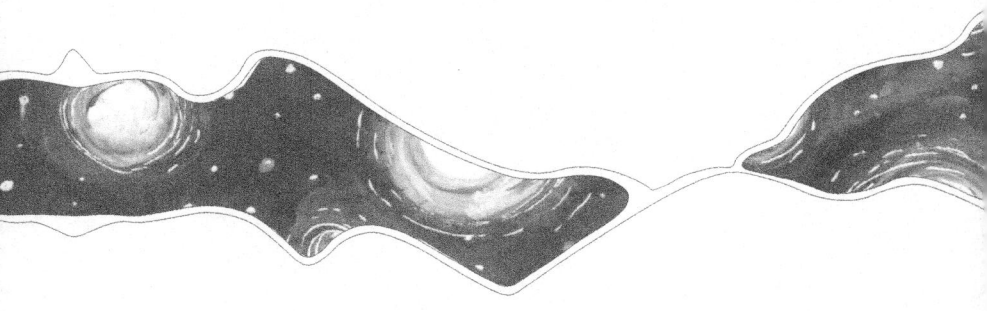

Is it an internal hollowness of despair
Or an external bullet;
Of being an anomaly, subdued aside
I wonder, what's the nothingness of void?

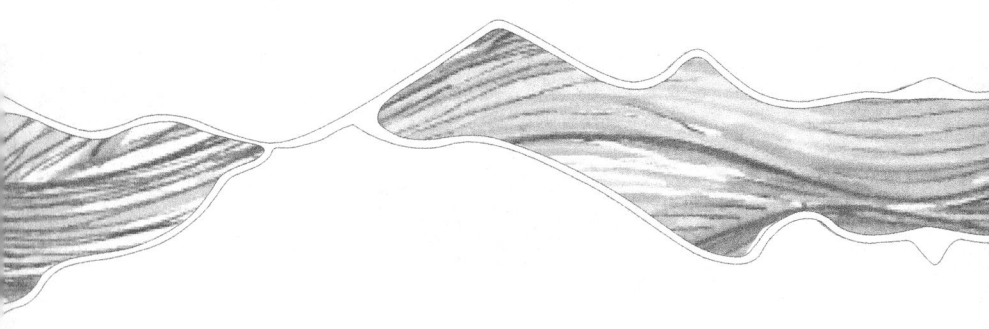

PIECES OF ME

It's been so long finding myself
looking in the mirror
waiting for the dots to connect
Not to be tricked by mind, so corrupt!

It's been so long finding myself
in people, I meet
in journeys I take
in the relationships I make.

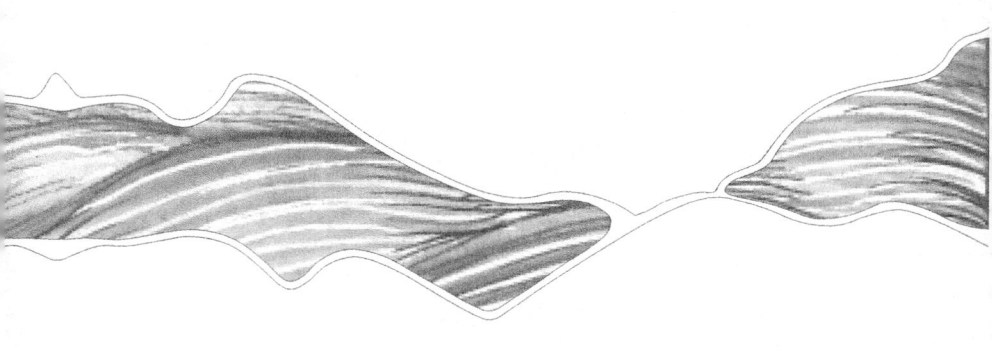

It's been so long finding myself
in a vacuum of thoughts
suffocating and choking soul
stuck in some kind of black hole

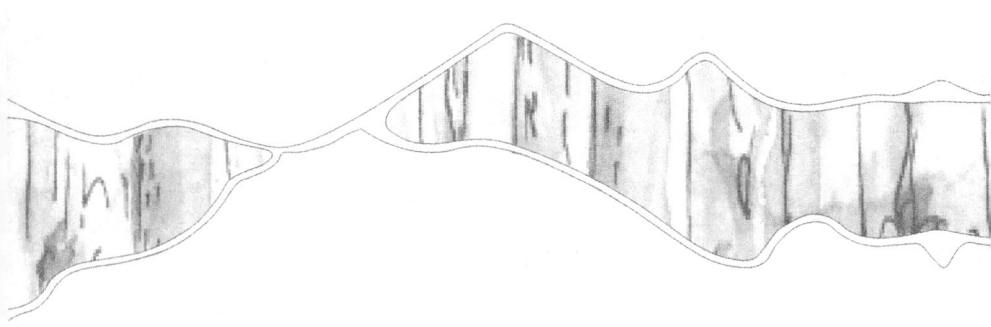

It's been so long finding myself
to solve a puzzle of my own pieces
As I lose my own shine,
Unable to keep track,
of my own little mind.

The world claiming to describe me better
than I do,
"Who am I?"
As I try to define
My broken parts
in some broken words
Repeatedly failing,
pieces of me, leisurely mending.

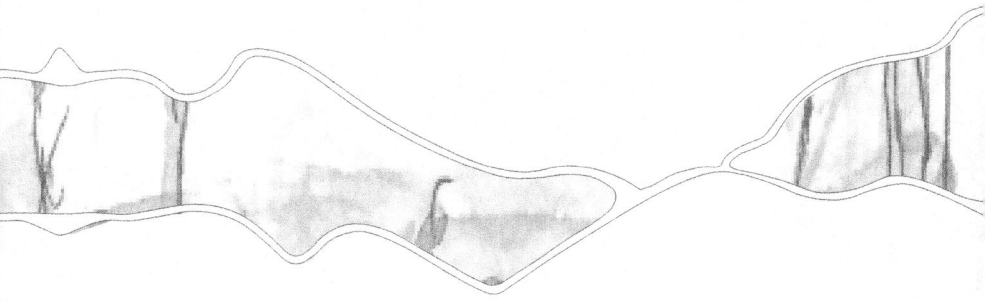

SEASONS

February made me shiver as I write
and their words cut me deep inside
Not to prove my love was not a lie
But to bleed is to know
Those feelings need to die

Rather, left the fight.
To be on that last flight
Hoping you would've called
The other night

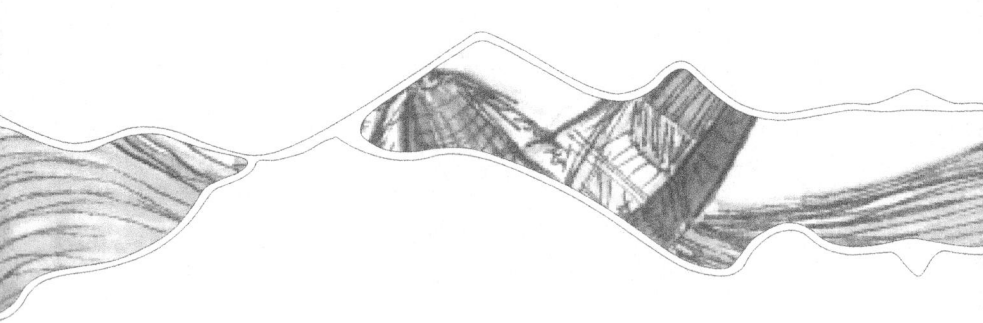

March, how many tears were shed
Under the moonlight
Without being noticed
Out of sight

Seasons changed; summers passed by
Occasionally, tearing up my eye
My hands scrolled through the screen

Reaching out to their names
My body sent chills all over again
How did it happen?
My heart ripped out in vain.

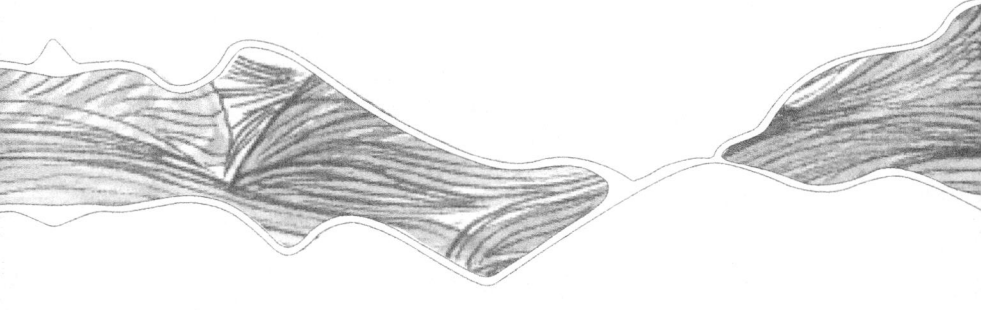

I was weeping willows
and nobody can see
All thanks to the atrocious August rain.

Cracks were there
as I missed pieces of my own
Slowly, steadily see myself gathering
To find it all over
as I stumbled upon your town
just to see a smooth criminal
in that crown.

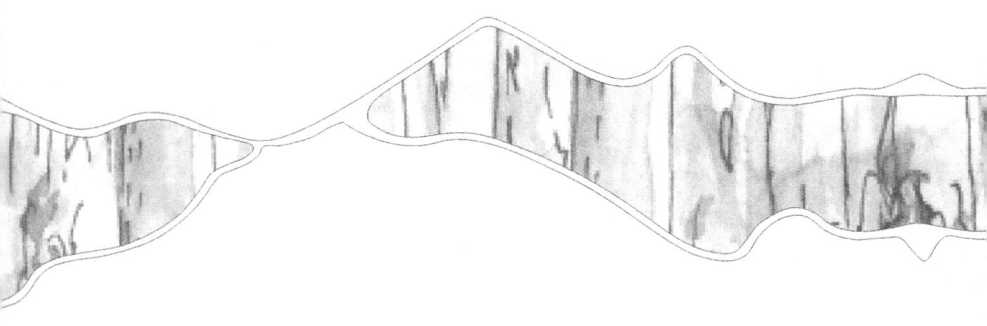

November, I thought I might
change the end of the story
But the cheeky winter
and glorious weather
My heart imagining
A festive December
Little did I know it was going to be
A cruel, cold winter.

And here I am again in January,
writing it all in my poetry

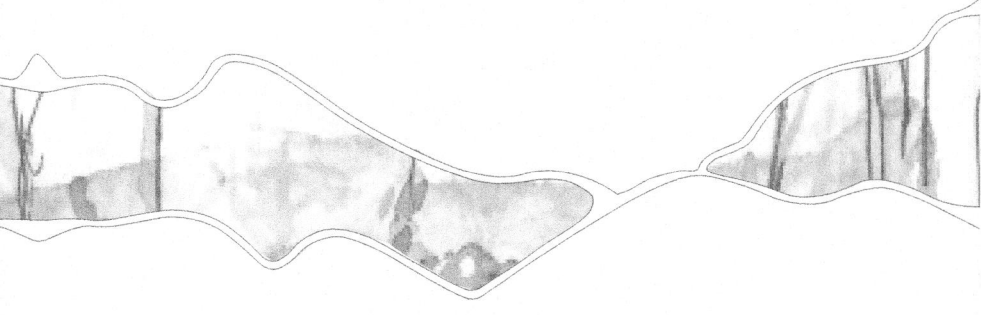

Love that never arrived on Christmas,
Neither to correct me nor to tell me what it was
ebb and flow of season's tide.
I chose a heart of stone, and in strength to abide
over maintaining a heart of glass, so fragile.

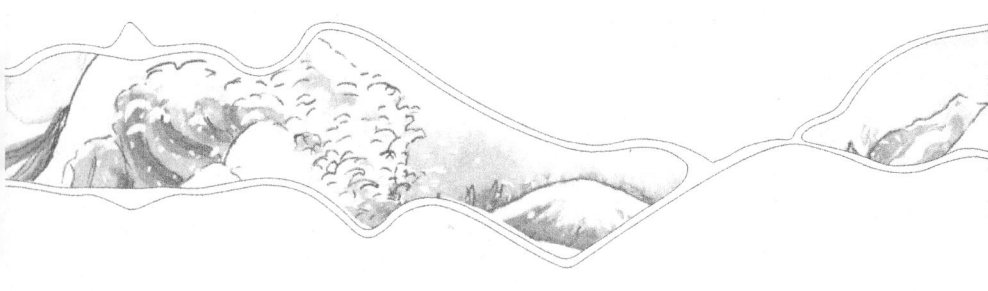

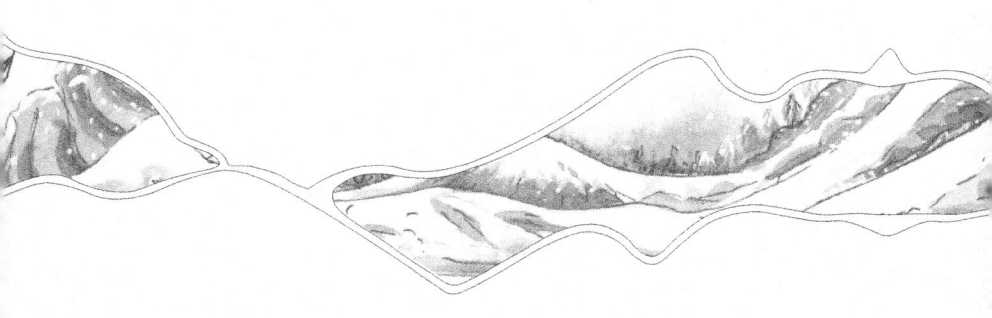

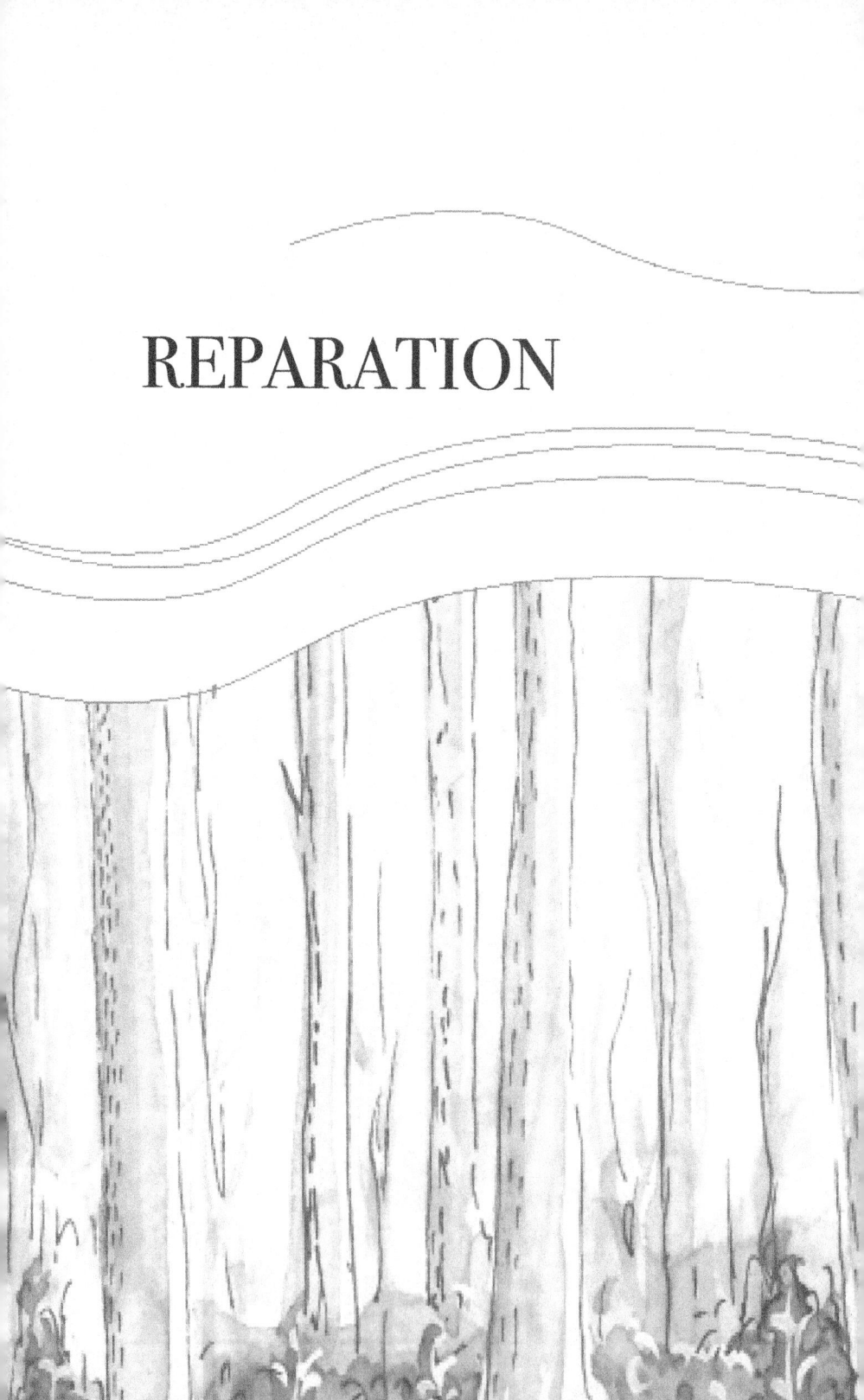
REPARATION

SLOW LOVE

Come when you're sure of me
Come when your mind isn't oscillating
Come when the stars go dim
and night at the brim
Come when it's intentional, and you know
you can love me slow

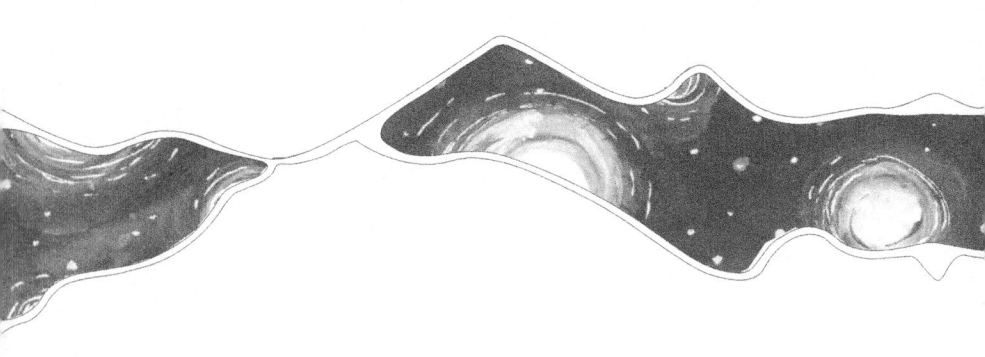

Come to hold me down
tight in your big arm
to hold me to dance
Come when you don't fear
To be the strength,
when I shed a tear
come when you can show
how you can love me slow

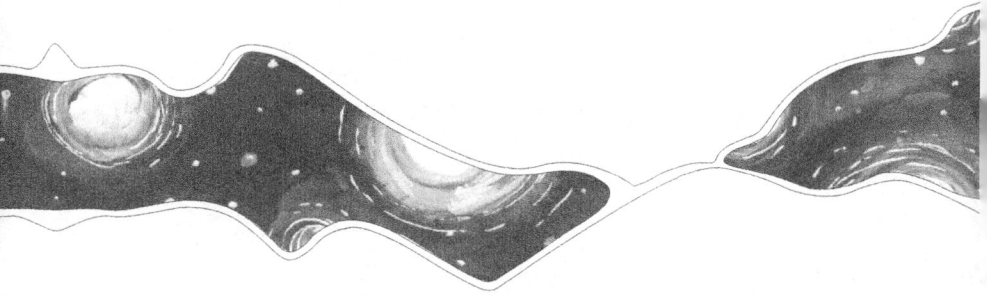

Come when you can see through my darkness
not just the outer light
Come when I am burning in the fire
this wild world ignites
Come to hug me tight,
In that broad daylight
Come as I age and more candles I blow
To get older while loving me slow

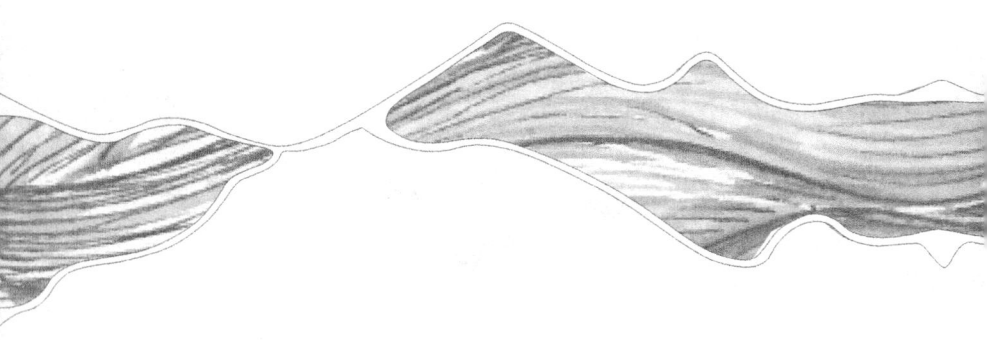

TO UNLOVE IS LOVE TAKING A STEP BACK

The constant struggle between
the mind and heart,
trying to discern past mistakes,
who was truly at fault?

Your promises to meet me halfway,
So, I donned rose-colored glasses,
in one way or another, letting life sway by.
All my time and love,
you expended like currency in the fray.

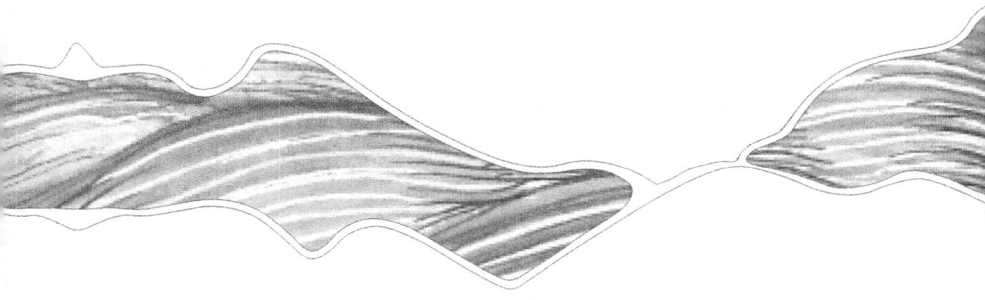

It took too long for me to know
My stubborn love and courage I show
Like a melting candle
In your thunderous storms,
You put me off in a single blow

How did I become a stone from a diamond?
How hard it was to mend
you'll never know, maybe, in your entire lifetime
As you never tried reading my silence
or anything between the lines.

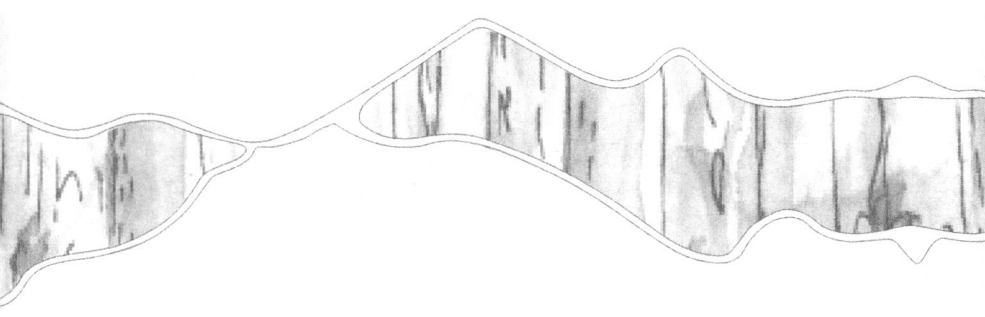

Here, I took from you your unseen scars,
Striving to fill them with my sparks.
Now I am left lying, longing,
For all that in me was once sparkling.

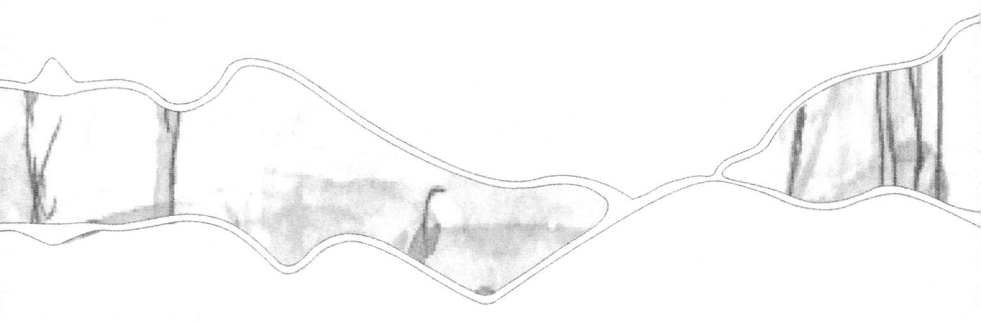

WHERE I DWELL

It was dead dark; I fell
It was a rough bark; I held
It's a story unheard, I tell

I took a deep breath; I propel
Looked down but did not dispel
It's a cocoon of love, I dwell

When I came out and rebel
I got bruised; I yell
It's a story unheard, I tell

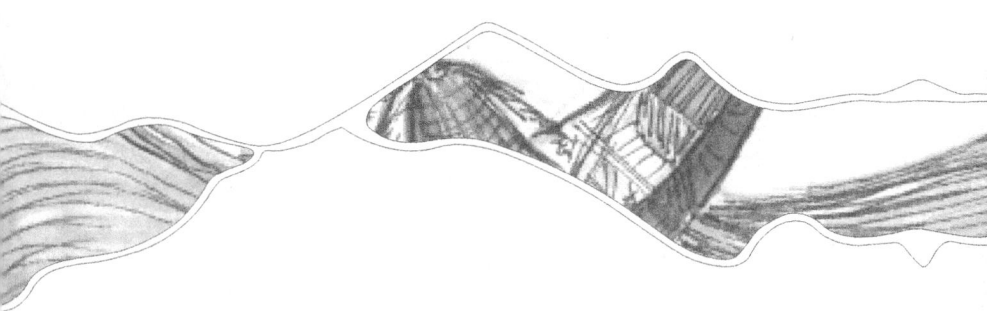

I picked myself from that hell.
It was a bad day; I compel
I went back to my cocoon; I dwell

I was scared, I retell
When it was dead dark, I fell
I looked back at my trail

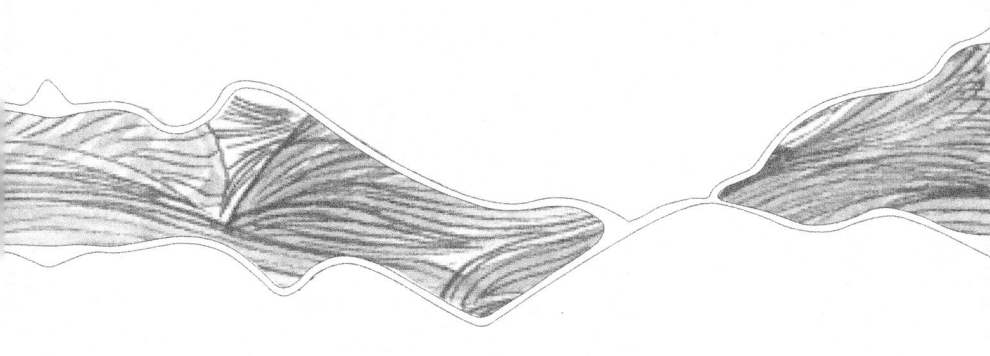

I was a strong survivor of that dell
Realized darkness wasn't the reason I fell
Lack of light, well.

I made my own lights and bell
Wind chimes and music, I sell
It's a cocoon of love I dwell

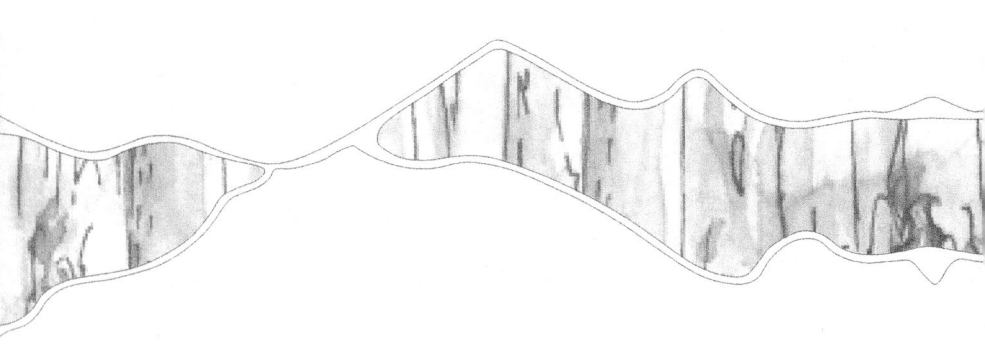

BREAK ME APART

Sometimes, I feel nothing can break me
or tear me apart
I wonder why
So, I rewind
To see how many times
I was being broken and
silently trying,
collecting little pieces to mend,

How many times I tried to fill up those cracks
with more and more glittery shiny glue,
like gold to Kintsugi

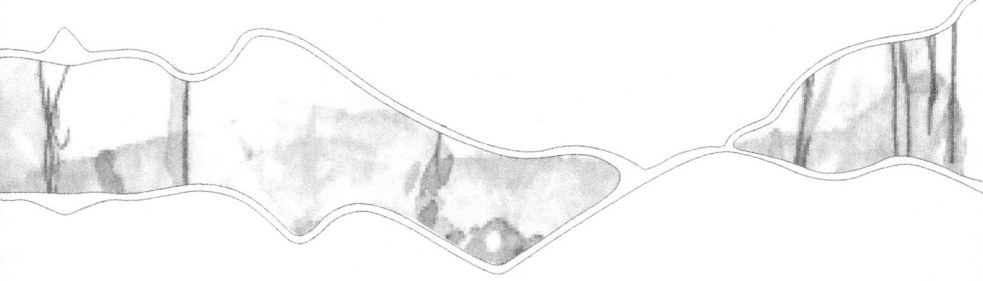

Every time, it seems even more surreal.
I try to comprehend,
Have I begun to love
The process of mend?

Perhaps to mend
those cracks generously
With wisdom and an expanding reality,
saving me from a future fatality.

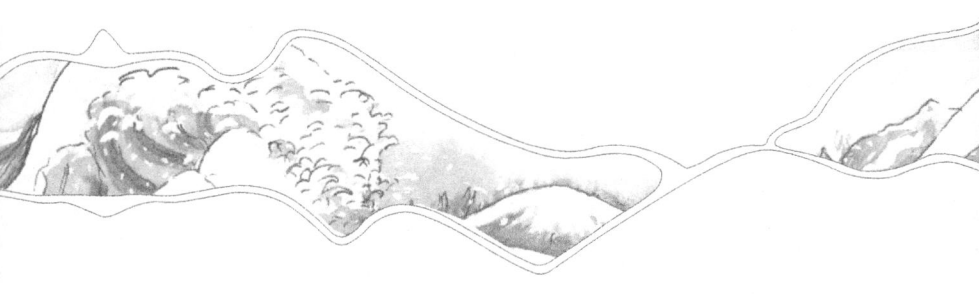

The toughness sensitizing
how easy it is to break.
A promise to self;
getting better to outshine
and strive to be stronger
than the last time

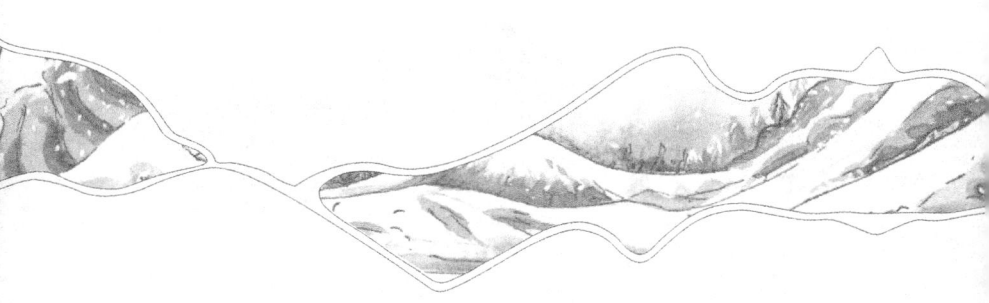

I wonder if I can ever be fixed like before,
As I shed parts of myself
Crushing, scrubbing
separating and recovering
like a diamond in its polishing

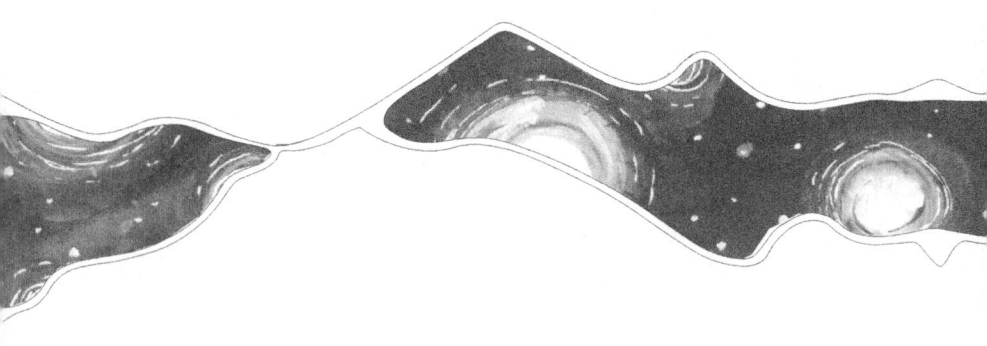

So, as I lose the fear
of breaking anymore
Slipping from my sleeves, my heart
What can possibly break me now
or tear me apart?

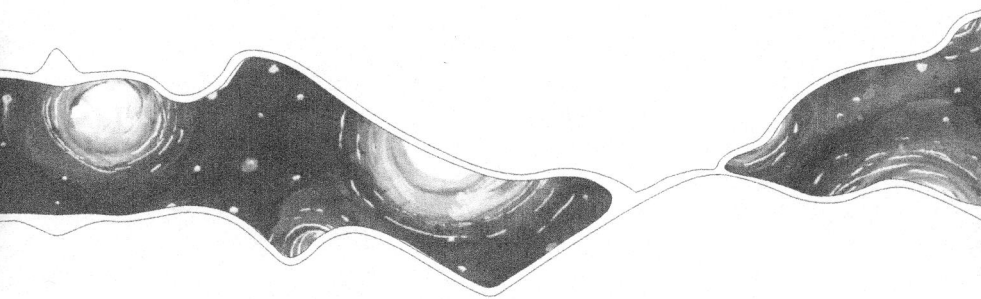

PREY

Dressing up on those nights
with garnishing of love,
lipstick and preppy smile

For him to feast on her beauty
Innocence and charm, tender sides
Like a phenomenon, so mala fide

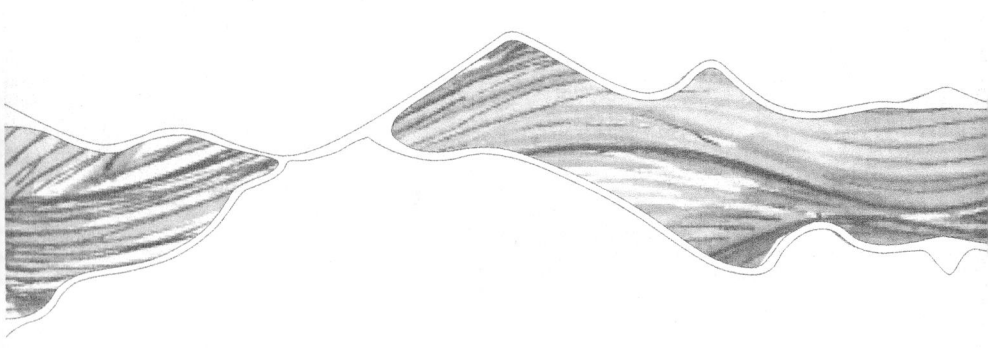

Consumed all her shine
For his dark appetite
Dining in the cage, he made
by his rules and recipes tonight

Too late for guts to listen
Till his taste buds become so indifferent
and he starts craving and praying
for some new obsession

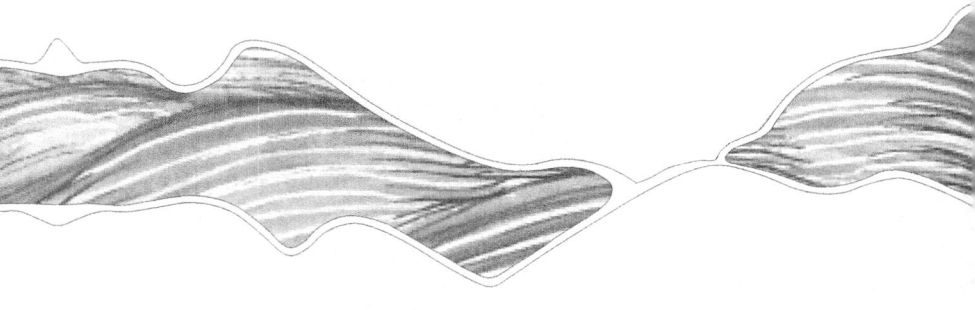

SHADOW TUNNEL

Tell me you liked getting spoiled
Or is it just me who like
flowers bit torn at the ends
I see more life to it
Is degeneration a new birth?

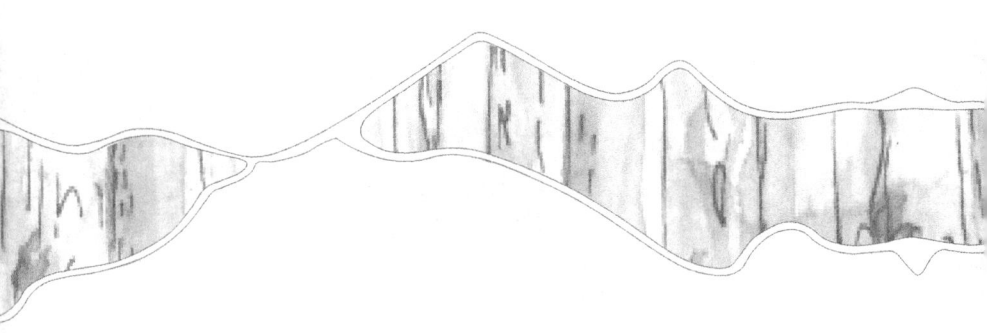

Tell me I'm not the only one walking through
this dark tunnel
To reach for the light of promises
I hope there's light in the end
Or I am seeing some kind the hollowness
Of your words?

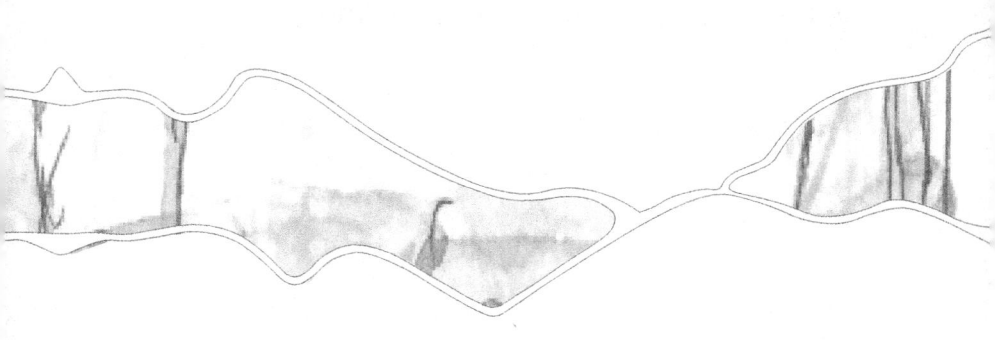

GREY

I see greys as lazy colors
Never want to be in extreme
tends to settle somewhere
Around nothingness of in-between

Grey escapes from commitments;
maybe they live in resentments.
They live in oblivion,
and never push themselves;
out of that land.
They say color of truth is grey;
I wonder if it can really take any stand.

BLACK AND WHITE

When I tried to read between those lines

Black pointed out
To the emptiness of white

White passed the buck
To the boldness of black

Both agreed on the same note

CAMOUFLAGE

POV SKIN

I still remember the touch
Of the ones who made love
Now left you, broke you,
So badly, like a deadly sin.
Let me introduce you to yourself better,
As I am your skin

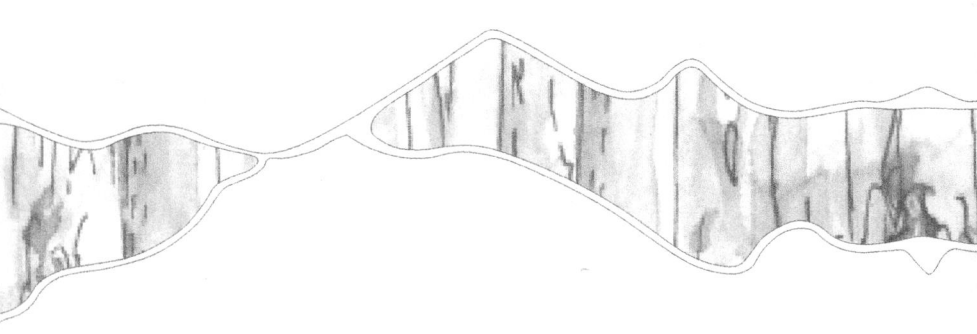

But you don't stop looking for light,
By keeping your heart open.
I know you're expanding your capabilities
To love, caught in commotion.
I know you're healing through each rising sun,
When I breathe your soul in every little win.
Trust me, I am your skin.

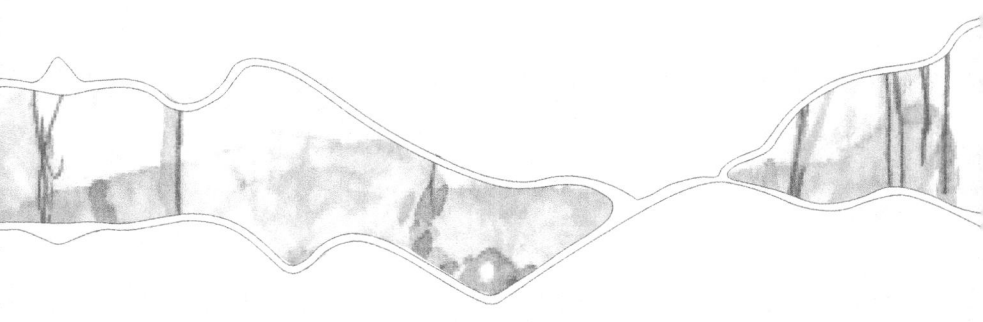

I know you're evolving each night out of undue influence,
in those vulnerabilities wrapped in a blanket,
hiding all the scars the world gave you.

Each night, I sleep with you and your pillow.

Teardrops washing me in the night glow
I watch you as you brim,

Silently, I am your skin.

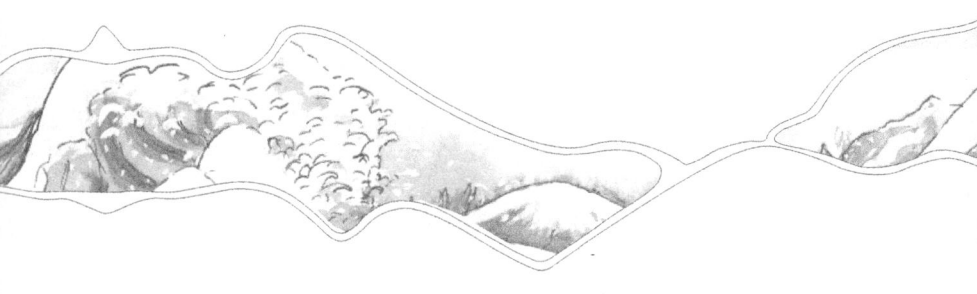

I know your pores are full of enigma,
but when you chase for perfecting them leaves
me in awe,
as little did you know you're most beautiful in
your raw,
Being true is not a sin,

Listen to me; I am your skin.

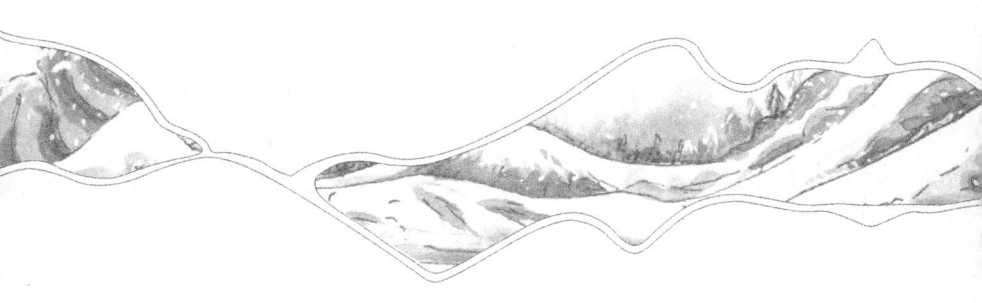

Those freckles, those scars,
those wrinkles, those cuts of the war,
I wear it on me

To show them your journey,
don't conceal the struggles that made you,
who you are
By making it so far.

I have it all on me written, tingling;
Like a journal, I am your skin.

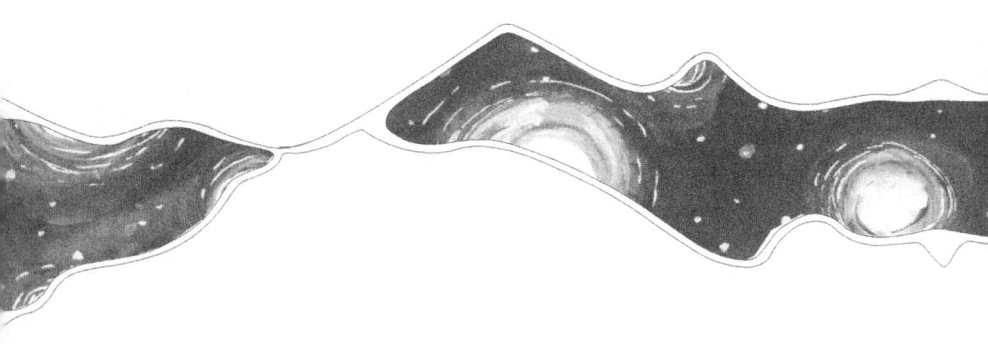

THE ASSEMBLY

To assemble is a craft
Gets better with practice

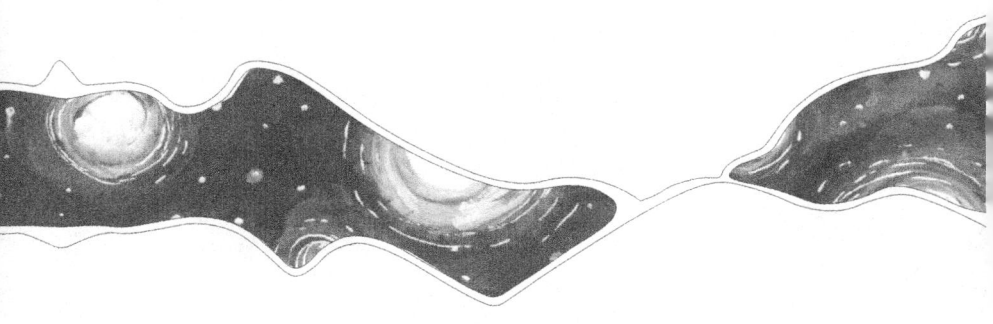

Honed and perfected with time.
I've realized, it comes to
us naturally;
often like a surreal gift,
offered lovingly by unseen hands.

Wrapped in old newspaper,
the rust of survival clings,
whispers of a broken past.
Right there we might need a pause,
To find space and look at
those vulnerable spots.

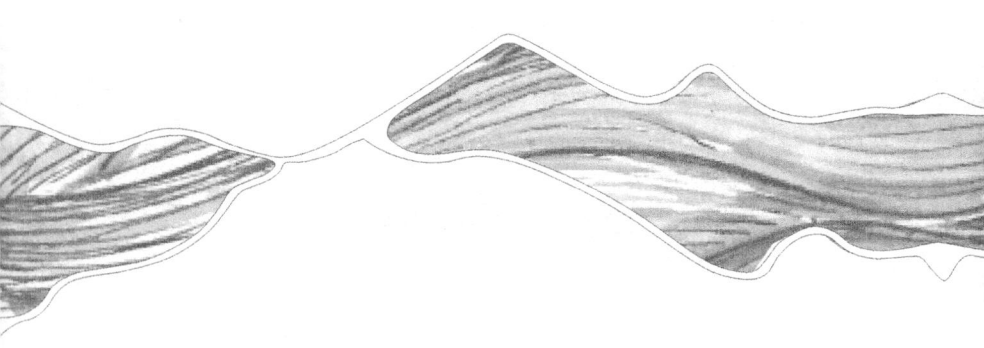

And you keep looking for the light
till you're in the making.
An assembly of soul,
is tedious and exhausting

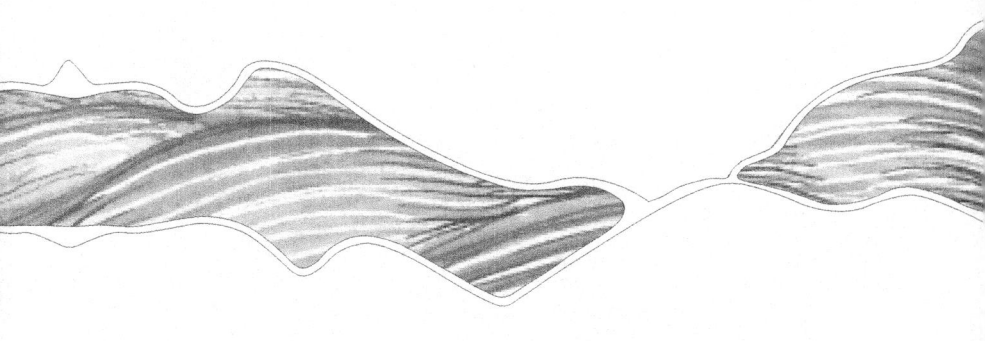

REPARATION

RESTORATION

MASK UNMASKED

Little did we know
we were given masks since we were born
Acting like an essential wear kit,
each to fit in wherever you want
Each for different occasions,
wear it, flaunt it, fit in
Just so easy, isn't it?

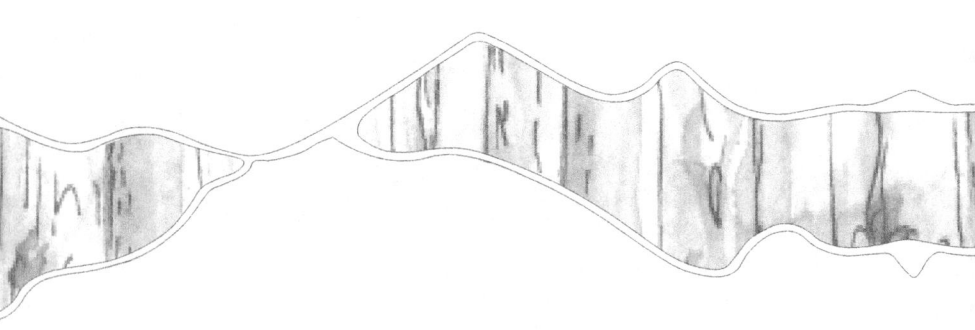

We took this hamper of an easy life
Changing it every little while;
Those masks help you walk in the crowd
And easily see eye to eye;
Announcing the same goals,
same success, that same old style

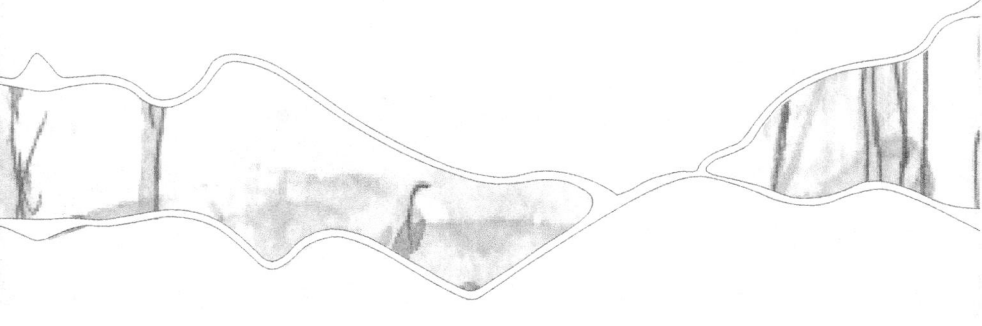

We started loving the idea
Of fitting in
without even knowing;

One not-so-fine day
the mask kit may get lost
And you'll hopefully ask
Mirror mirror, where's my mask?
"Can't you walk one day without?"
Mockingly, he'll ask.

Terrified soul choked to Answer,
too afraid to be real
And get unmasked
Holding that dark, dread reality
Caught in duality
Acting, hiding morality
slipping inside the case.

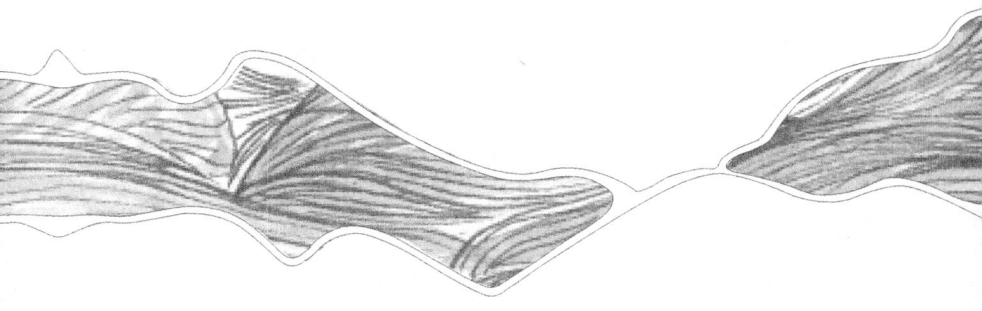

Only one day when the show is over
Too late to realize
How a soul beneath the mask
already died crippling inside!

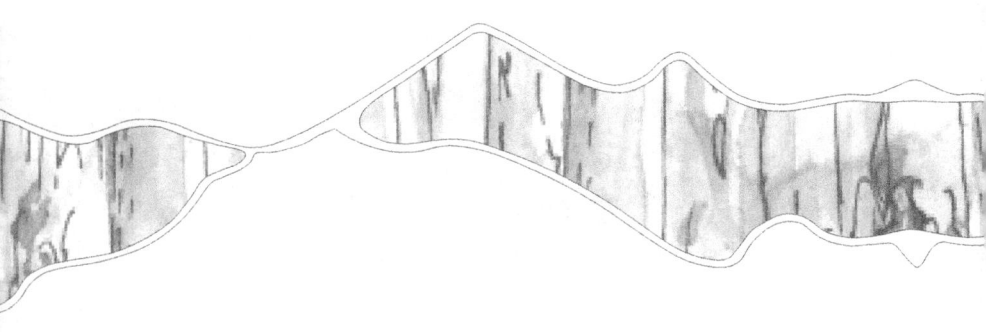

HATE LETTER

Dear love,

Chaos and fire
Never someone's desire
To bury deep in the state of troubles
Or too handicapped to share
In the nick of time, when life passes us by
Awaiting all conversations, hellos and goodbyes

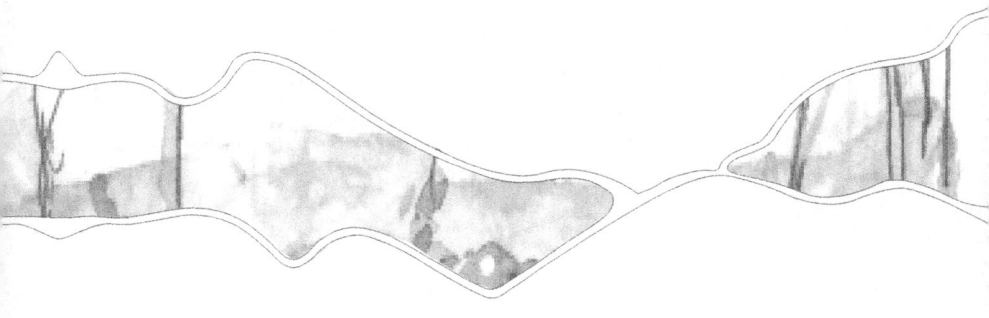

How many bridges you'll burn
How many lovers you'll ruin
With no moss, one rolling stone
Your claims of being clean
And denied troubled waters were seen

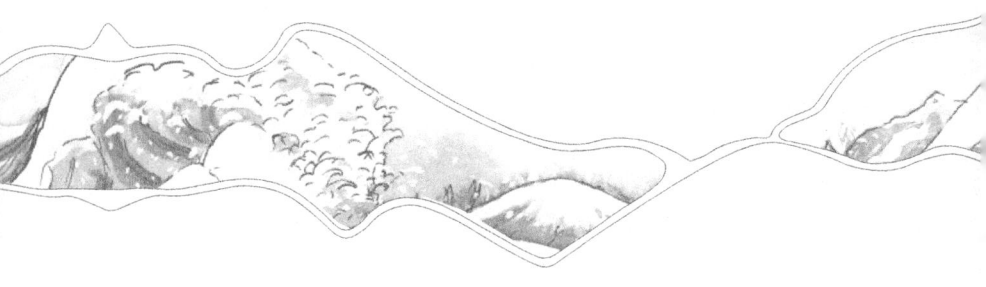

When I dreamt of you last night
Waking up terrified
How close I got to you
Even in my sleep, I apologize
Have I known you for some days
or those years of nightmares
How will I lie to myself and be mean
That troubled waters were seen

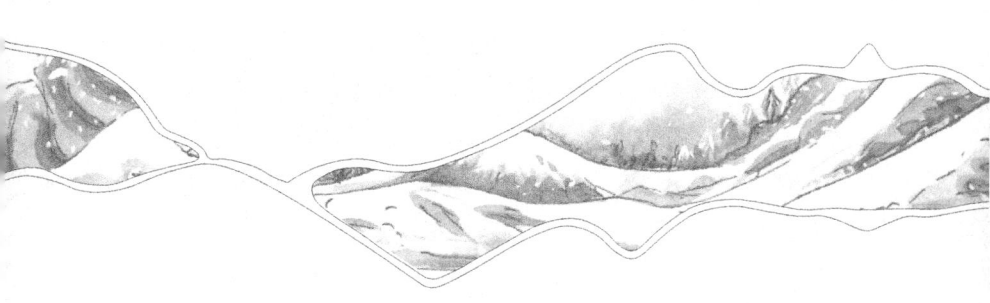

Every day, when I hold the tsunami
Of emotions and unsaid turmoil
That makes me questions
Do I still love you
Or is it the oceans I boil?

How would you know the struggle of survival
in troubled water
So, I'll describe you in a vivid poetry
and like I did in this letter

Yours lovingly

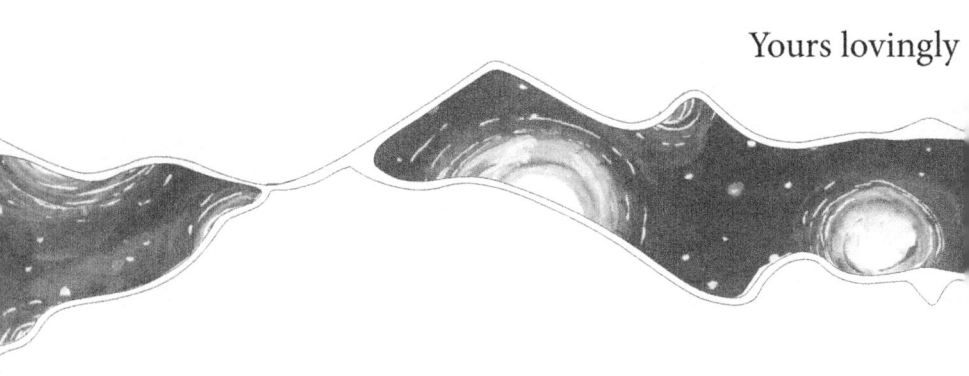

REIGNITE HOPE

There can't be any relationship that guarantees
 you to be with you forever.
There is no constant than your inner being
you spend your whole life with

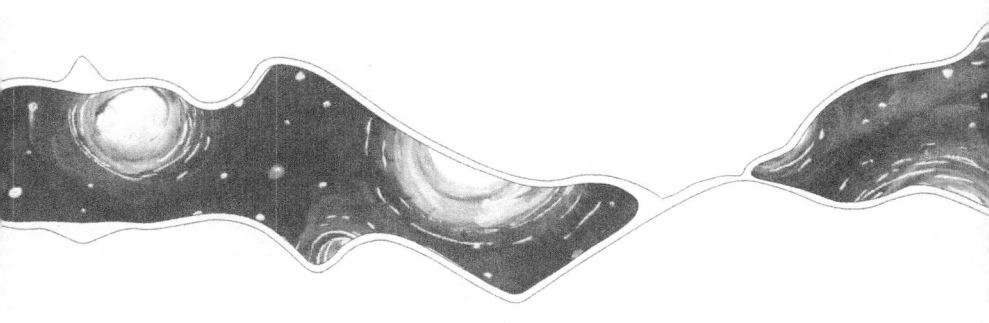

There will be a day
When times will get rough,
and troubled water you might sail
Your fingers quickly scrolling
to those SOS numbers
Just to hear: "Please drop a voicemail."

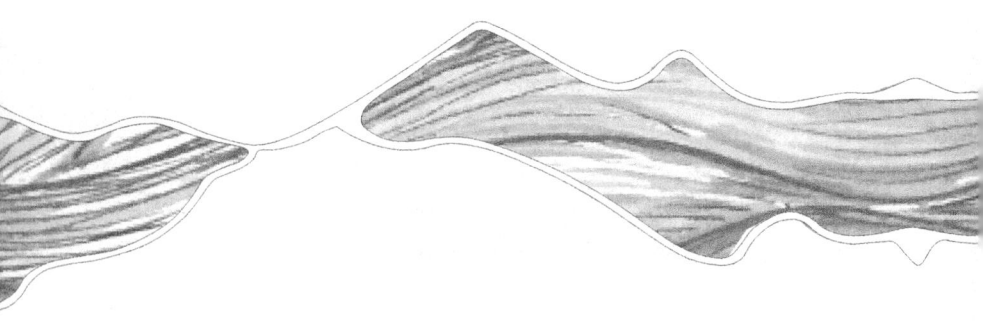

But you can't lose hope,
but shed your skin for new realities
and still believe in those cinematic relationships
where endings are happy, and love is pure,
eternal, ethereal and for whom, they're sure!

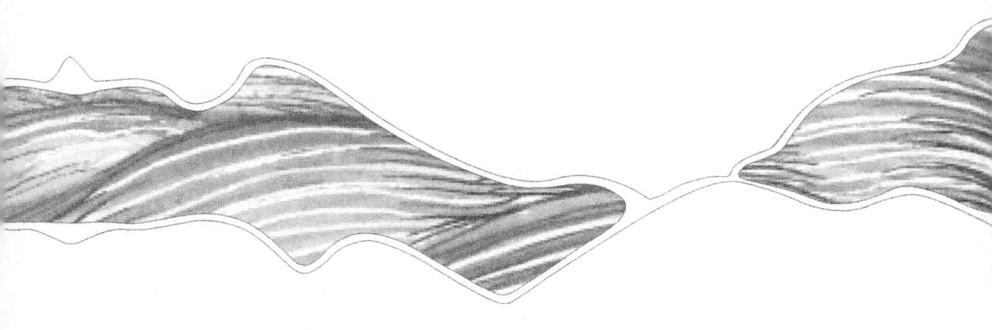

Even that's not everyone's story
but we need someone's story to pass on
to set exemplar
and tell the world
how to love better.

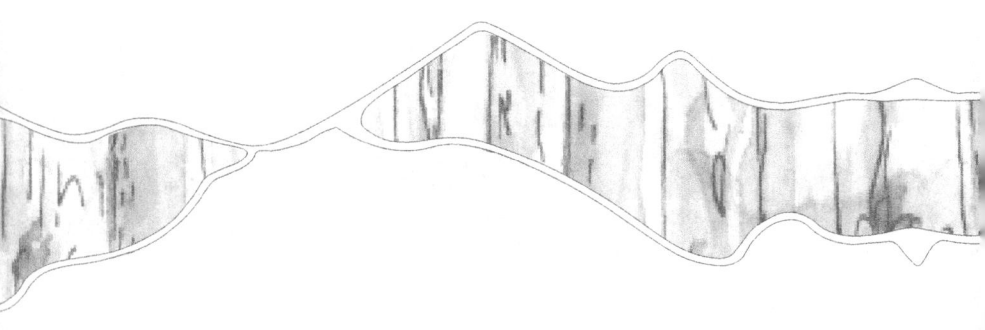

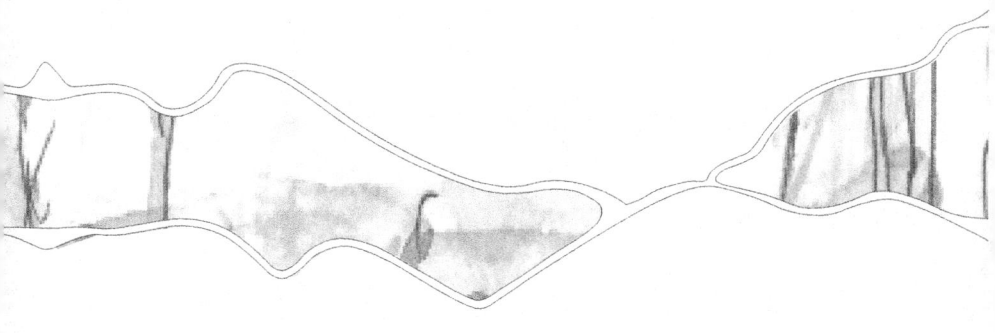

RESTORATION

PERFECTING IMPERFECTIONS

Like divinely created flowers with irregular
petals
The brown bark with perfect knots
of slightly bent shafts
of that not-so-perfect tree
The glory of sunset with an imperfect
circumference
and of light that glee

The geometry of God wasn't a circle
but an endless spiral
Opponents in my head
with debating thoughts so chiral
As I try to know the perfect curve
Infinity gets on my nerve

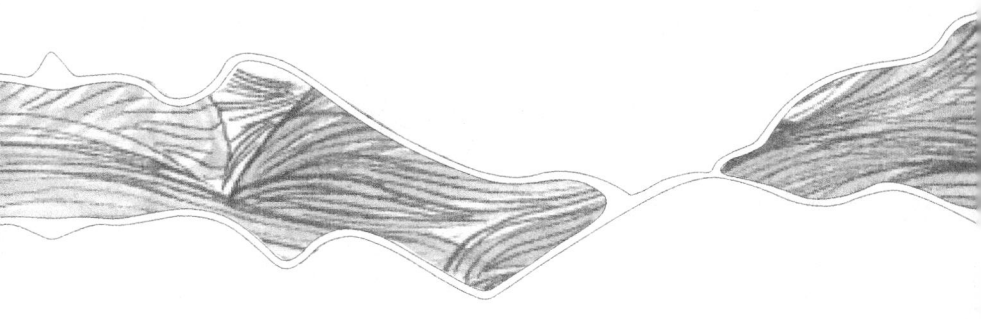

Blooming lilies never argue
about who's perfect in their view
each of them exists to bless the world in a different color
Wonder! What's the chase from others to be better

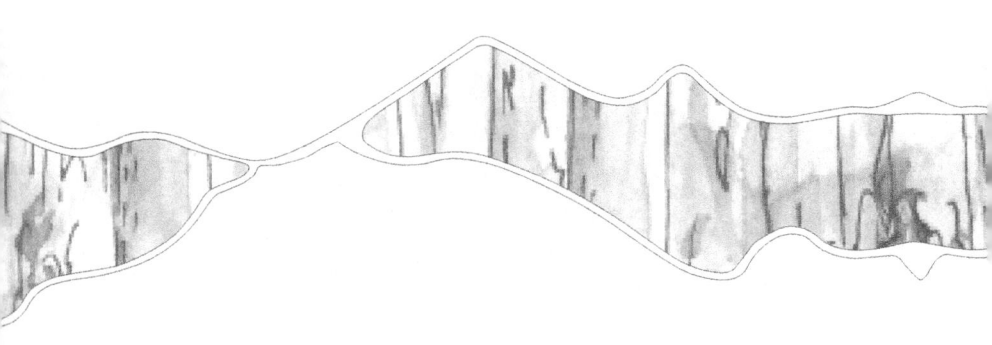

With all the great things that
comes with some surreal mess
I am finding perfection
in such imperfectness

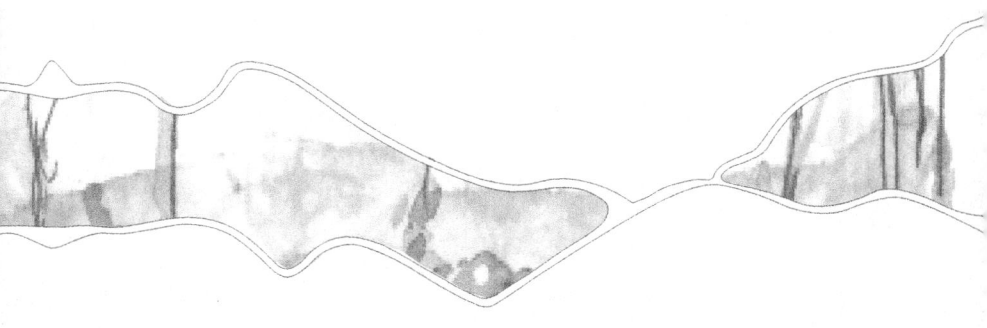

JOINERIES

Perfecting life, like kintsugi,
shutting all the gaps, rebuilding my joineries,
I weave my hopes in poems and some songs,
Breaking from curses that lingered so long.

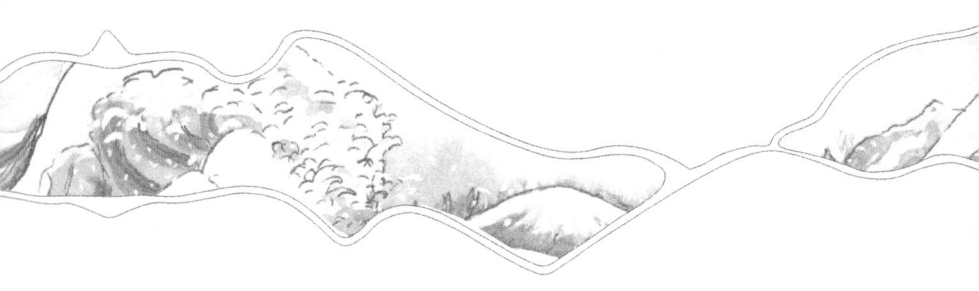

Stubborn dreams and persistence, my ally
Filling my cracks with glimmers,
crevices to crucify.
Traits of innocence and naivety,
Like a child blind to the world's depravity.

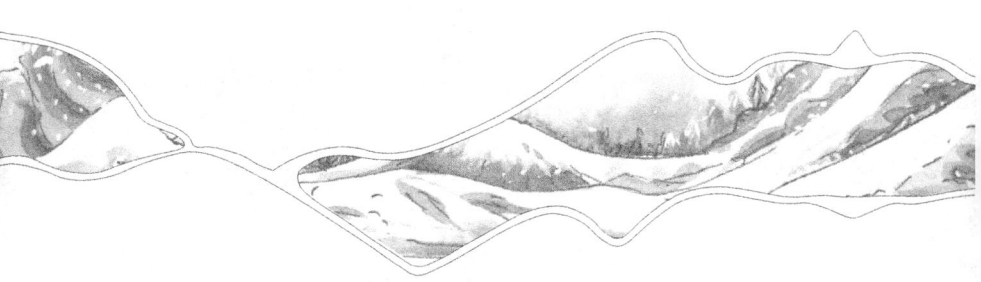

REMINSCENTS

Seasons changed, lessons learned,
Like a flower growing amongst thorns;
Promises of sunshine and storms.
Hoping to see a brighter sky,
Once clouds of despair have passed us by.

I looked back in reminiscence,
Or was I just trying to live a lie?

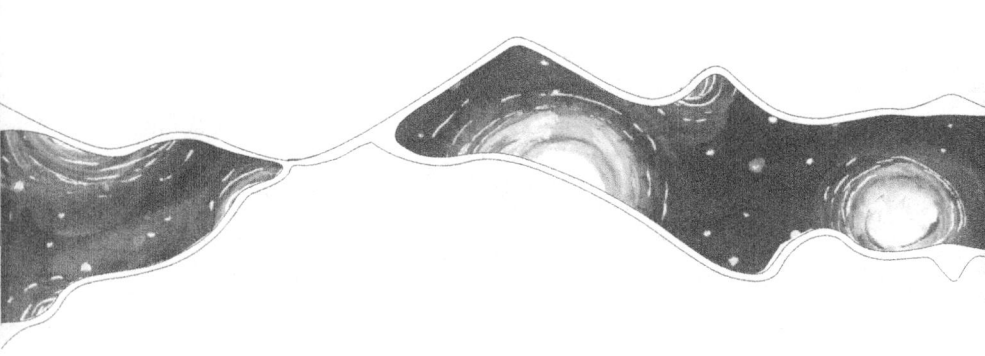

TO MY AMBIVALENT DEMONS

The pain which can make me numb
eventually to become a weapon
to rise above & conquer
my ambivalent demon

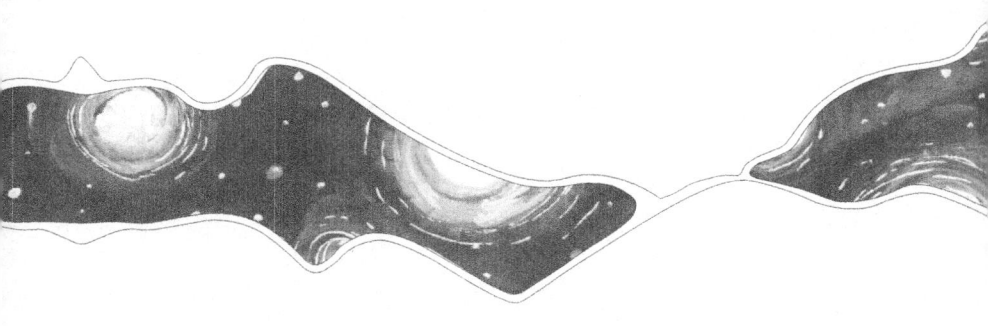

To feel pity or to cry on scarcity
was never an acceptance of my integrity
So, chose to deny, be happily delusional
to generations that shamed me
for my dreams, big enough to be

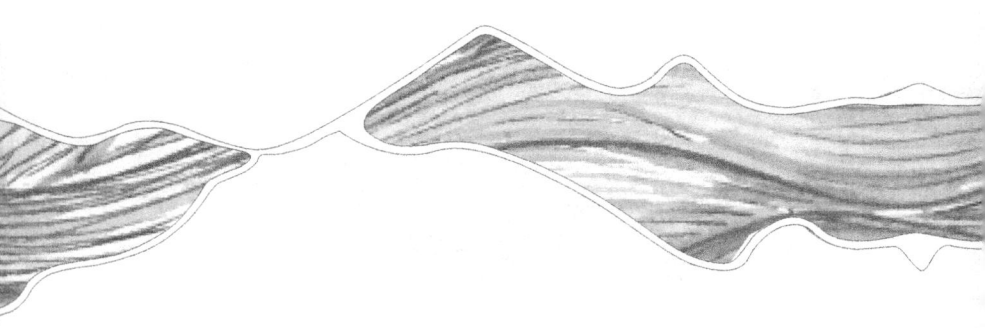

They lowered the curtains on my rising sun,
Feeding on the insecurities of what I could become.
Gradually, the shadows may grow darker,
But my light will shine even brighter

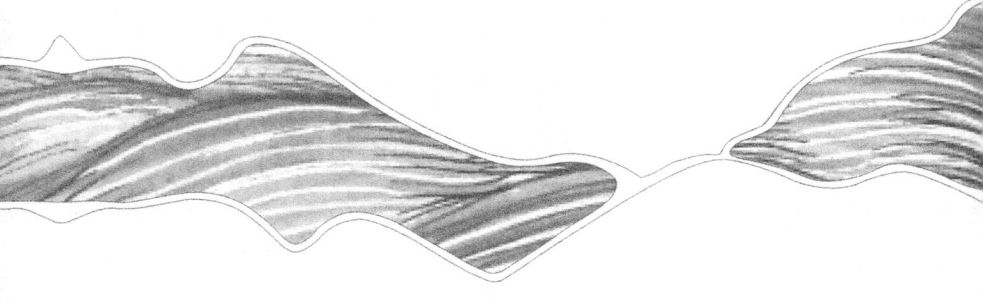

To be grateful for tears
pulling out ace cards on all my fears
buried under the dark of night, rather than rantings
to being just needed luminosity of my paintings

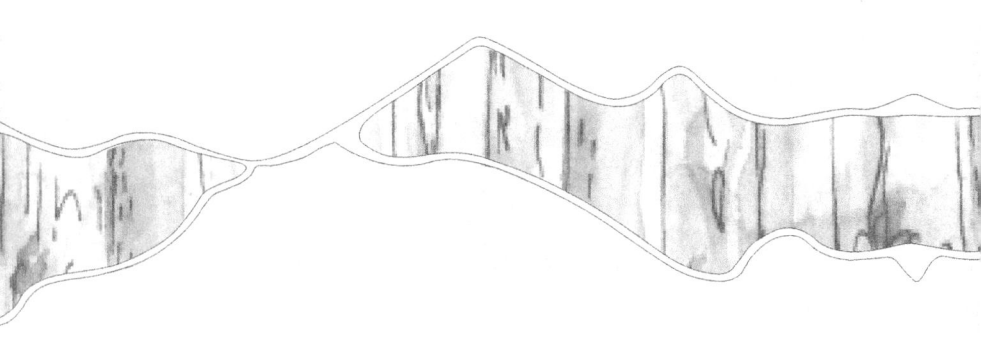

So, here I choose not to sulk and surrender to despair
but to peel every brittle, harsh, unfulfilling layer
of myself, to adapt, evolve in new skin
not ageing but eternally growing

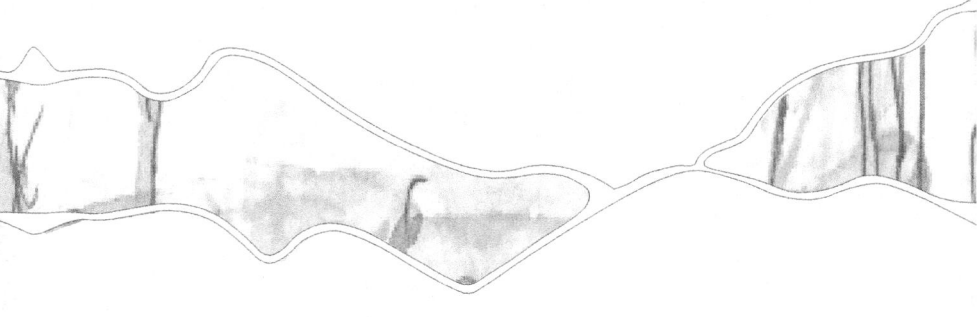

To respect and love every piece of energy
given by a gigantic galaxy
knowing my demons to know my divinity
till it takes it back to give to another entity!

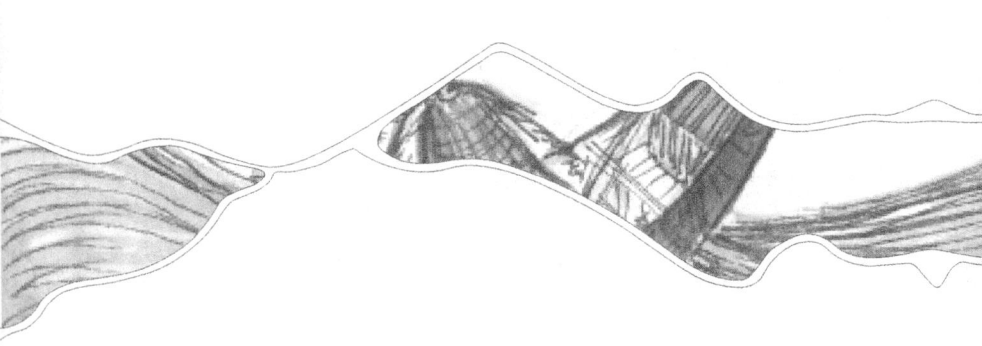

Perfection is merely an idea built on perceptions.
Here's to not losing the authenticity of imperfections.

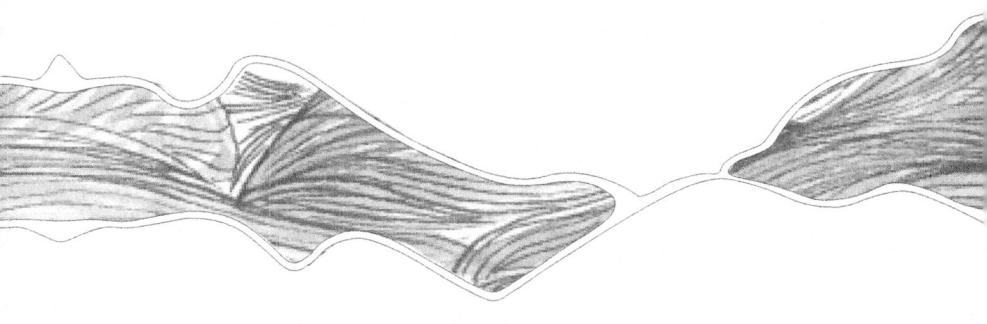

Made in the USA
Monee, IL
03 May 2026

49438947R00066